CROSSINGS

CROSSINGS

A Journey Through Borders

Nicholas Murray

Seren is the book imprint of
Poetry Wales Press Ltd.
57 Nolton Street, Bridgend, Wales, CF31 3AE
www.serenbooks.com
facebook.com/SerenBooks
twitter@SerenBooks

The right of Nicholas Murray to be identified as
the author of this work has been asserted in accordance
with the Copyright, Designs and Patents Act, 1988.

© Nicholas Murray, 2016

ISBN: 978-178172-347-0
ebook: 978-1-78172-348-7
Kindle: 978-1-78172-349-4

A CIP record for this title is available from the British Library.

The publisher acknowledges the financial assistance of the Welsh Books Council.

Printed by Latimer Trend, Plymouth.

*I am grateful to Literature Wales for a Writer's Bursary in 2013 which enabled
me to write this book.*

Contents

Preface

Contemporary global politics are dominated by the worldwide refugee crisis. The UN High Commissioner for Refugees estimates that there are more than sixty million forcibly displaced people worldwide. Over four million of these have come from Syria alone, to be added to refugees from Afghanistan and Iraq.

The arrival of the refugees – desperate, hungry, ill, abused by people traffickers and harried by every sort of official authority – has provoked many spontaneous acts of generous welcome but also some hateful scenes. Catholic bishops in Poland have been heard to proclaim that Muslim migrants bring disease and threaten to destroy what they call Latin civilisation. Racists have been on the march across Europe as well as in the United States. In Hungary a 110-mile razor-wire wall was erected last autumn closing the country's southern frontier with Serbia. In Calais six thousand refugees have survived a winter in slum camps known as The Jungle.

Never since the end of the Second World War has the existence of political borders, and the pressure on them from migrants, been more starkly highlighted in a Europe itself divided and uncertain about its own sense of itself, something that is confirmed by the current debate about Britain's continued membership of the European Community.

This book is in no sense an attempt to address that crisis directly but tries to explore the idea of borders – literal and metaphorical – and what the concept of drawing lines of demarcation between countries, cultures, classes, languages, regions means. Why do we erect borders? What needs do they fulfil? Can we do without them? It is not an academic thesis but draws on personal experience, anecdote, literary and imaginative sources to cross and re-cross our idea of the border, of the dividing lines, margins, barriers, limits, thresholds, liminal spaces, exclusive categories that we erect between ourselves and others or even inside ourselves.

I live in border country, in the Welsh Marches, where these concepts have a local habitation and a name. To me the concept of liminality is not an abstract or theoretical one. It is something I think I have lived out in my life. As the wonderfully sardonic Albanian author Gazmend Kapllani puts it in his *A Short Border Handbook*: 'In the final analysis, we are all migrants, armed with a temporary residence permit for this earth, each and every one of us incurably transient.'★

Kinnerton, Powys,
March 2016

★ *A Short Border Handbook* (Portobello Books, 2009) by Gazmend Kapllani trans Anne-Marie Stanton-Ife

Part One: Crossings

1. Dreams Dry Up

Melilla. A tiny thumbprint of Spain on the coast of North Africa. It is the night before my departure by ferry for Melilla and I am in a bar in Malaga, in one of the back streets away from the main tourist area. Malaga is the most popular tourist destination in Spain after Barcelona. Nearly a million people visit the city each year, most on their way to the Costa del Sol. It even has a 'tourism czar' called Elias Bendodo whose job involves making important statements like "golf is a key element in the battle against the seasonal nature of tourism." Elias and his bureau for tourism claim credit for the impressive visitor statistics, and for the fact that people are not just passing through on their way to the Costas. They are increasingly staying for a day or more to see the city's "cultural offerings" which in my case consists of some seemingly effortless but enchanting drawings by Picasso in the museum dedicated to him.

I am up at the bar trying to order a glass of *vino tinto* but the barmaid is deep in a voluble, seemingly unstoppable riff with another customer so I tap my feet on the floor and inspect the tapas. Is that pale stuff under a plastic cover tripe? Eventually she sees me from the corner of her eye and, making a pacifying gesture with her outstretched arms to her interlocutor, comes over to ask me what I want. Hearing my English-accented Spanish she launches now into another riff delivered in perfect Estuarial English about the weather and a range of other breathless topics. It turns out that she spent a portion of her childhood in Essex. I decide to take advantage of this to ask her a question about something that has been bothering me all day.

"When I studied Spanish in school for "O" Level we were told to pronounce "*Gracias*" as "Grathias".

She wipes the counter absently with a cloth then whisks an empty glass into the sink. She is not sure where this conversation is going or why it was started.

"Yes?"

"Well, the check out girls at the El Corte Inglès supermarket all say "Grassia".

She lets out a short, crisp sound, halfway between a laugh and a snort.

"In fact everyone seems to say "Grassia", dropping the final 's' and not softening the 'c' with the tip of the tongue in the way I was taught."

She waves her hand dismissively and impatiently in the air then smacks a glass of *tinto* down on the zinc.

"Oh, we're all Cockneys down here!"

Next day, late in the afternoon, I board the nearly empty ferry from Malaga to Melilla. Sea journeys, whatever the weather, always raise my spirits. This, I always feel, is real travel. The smack of a sharp breeze, the rough feel of salt drying on the handrail, the rumble of engines far below, streaks of rust on the hull. It's true I have had it rough in the Bay of Biscay, and even in the Aegean in the wrong sort of weather, but I can always console myself with the thought that things could be much worse. I could be on an aeroplane.

The ferry arrives late at night. It is dark, wet and windy. A bleak Sunday evening in December is not the perfect time to arrive in North Africa with no hotel booked. As one doubtful establishment after another turns out to be closed or full (unlikely as that seems) I eventually come to a halt outside a seedy hotel that looks promising – in the sense of being likely to offer a room. It is the kind of hotel that I used to stay in as a student backpacker and there's no reason to think I can't do so again as I'm always happy to rough it if I have to. And we are all too fussy these days about hotel rooms. All these unconvincingly smooth rationalisations are helped by the knowledge that it is late and I will be leaving early. But that carpet worries me. I don't think I will like the look of it when I see it in the morning in natural light. For the time being I am helped by the fact that there is a problem with the lights, both in the common areas and in the room itself, and the building is dank and cold. I tell myself, however, that this will have to do.

The next problem is food. Another half hour scouring the wet streets brings me to an almost empty, almost closed, bar that reluctantly holds off putting up the shutters to produce a snack that I can eat.

Next morning I am up early – and, yes, that foul green carpet is something I am reluctant to tread on in bare feet now that I have its measure in daylight. As soon as possible I catch a local bus, a short ride to the squalid border crossing, where the scene is one of mud and pools of rainwater. Some sort of desultory market is going on – improvised boxes and trays are set up in the midst of rubbish and filth – and a line of people from the Moroccan side are being channelled through a narrow passage whose sides consist of rusty iron bars that make the men and women look like caged animals waiting to be processed.

In fact, I think of the livestock market at Knighton on the Welsh border where, at the end of the weekly sale, men in long green wellingtons and boiler-suits hose away the oozy olive-green sheep manure from the concrete floor after the animals have been driven away in trucks.

These are the sub-Saharan migrants, desperate to get across the border to Spanish territory. In September 2005 they lost patience and stormed the fences. Seven hundred of them are said to have broken through, but six died at the hands of Moroccan security forces. Several fences have been built by the Spanish government here, each progressively stronger, to keep back the insistent human swell. The one they erected after 2005 was made of razor wire and cost 33 million euros. More than six miles of parallel fences, three metres high, enclosing a service road, were built. Later, the height had to be doubled when the migrants discovered they could shin over using home-made steps. Less visible are the underground cables, sensors, video cameras and all the customary electronic paraphernalia of surveillance.

Morocco does not like this fence. It does not recognise the Spanish claims to sovereignty over Melilla. The Spanish presence is a stain on the map of North Africa that the Moroccan government would like to see wiped off. Spain argues back that these territories have been an integral part of Spain since the fifteenth century, long before Morocco gained its independence from France. Periodic attacks, into the early 20th Century, from Rif Berbers have harried its borders but the population shows no sign of wanting any change from Spanish control. The last remaining statue of General Franco in Spain still stands here, but very recently Melilla (together with Ceuta, the other Spanish city enclave on this coast) turned the Muslim feast day of Eid into an official public holiday. Not since the *Reconquista* has a non-Christian religious festival received an official stamp of approval in this way in Spain.

Stepping aside to avoid a pool of muddy water, I join the queue at the border post. I do not have to wait very long because the traffic is all in the opposite direction.

The sour-faced passport official who reads the statement of my profession on the entry *fiche* demands aggressively what kind of *écrivain* I am and what I write for.

"*Des journaux?*"

"*Non, études littéraires.*"

I am cautious, having read that journalists are treated with suspicion in Morocco. This is a couple of years before the Arab Spring of 2011.

He pulls a face, crossly taps the passport on the sill, scribbles something, grunts, hands it back to me and turns his attention to someone else. I conclude that I can walk on. I am, after all, a white European male and I am going *into* Morocco.

On the other side, the taxi-drivers are waiting to take me to the nearest town where I will catch a long distance bus. But they would like that further business too and my chosen driver touts furiously as we drive along through the muddy landscape. On either side one sees so many young males with absolutely nothing to do, sitting about in complete immobility, slumped against a tree on a piece of waste ground even in this cold, wet weather.

There is a way of arranging one's limbs that conveys an impression of total abjectness.

★

Borders, I reflect yet again, are not attractive places. They want to instruct you, as forcefully as they can, about their importance, about what they signify, so everything about them is designed to underscore that meaning, if not rub your nose in it. There is no breeziness, no spirit of *laissez-faire* at a frontier crossing. Aggression, short temper, everything in the bully's box of tricks seem privileged at the border post. You have no automatic right to cross from one territory to another, say the custodians of the liminal fence, and it is necessary again and again to remind you of that salient fact. Especially if the pigment of your skin is not the one liked by the people on the other side of the border.

Humiliation, condescension, a cold, haughty arrogance, have always been the style of choice at border crossings, even when there is absolutely no need for it. When we cross borders today each of us is already listed on multiple computers, every passenger repeatedly documented by the airlines, checked and re-checked, and *still* it is necessary that we are made to feel uncomfortable, mildly irritated, docketed, looked at askance as if it were our sly intention to try it on, to make an illicit entry.

It doesn't have to be like this and in fairness there are many crossings where it isn't done in the old way. There are border officials who have found the way to be amiable. It can be done. But there is a residual culture of low-level hostility, of suspicion, of *unfriendliness*. A default setting of frigidity.

At Prague airport in the late 1980s a metal container in my luggage activated some sort of warning light or sensor. A uniformed official gestured languidly with his head that I should open my bag for inspection. His thin lips pursed in an expression of distaste, he started to pull out the contents of my bag with his immaculately white-gloved hands. The look of displeasure on his face grew as he, and the passing file of curious airline passengers, examined thoroughly the baggage. He pulled out each item, very slowly and gingerly, as if it were something rancid or toxic, foul-smelling, dubious. Then, on a sudden impulse he turned away, presenting me with his back. He was bored. The bag no longer interested him. Embarrassed, humiliated, I started to stuff the scattered items back into my bag. He would have learned his trade in the Communist era when treating with respect those who were not in petty positions of authority would have seemed a waste of effort, a practical absurdity. He was perfectly cast in his present job.

Borders, fairly obviously, de-limit, circumscribe, fence, define a piece of territory. They keep it in but they also keep out intruders, pretenders, invaders. The act of defining a border is inherently a hostile one; it wants you to know not merely that this patch is green, ringed with a red perimeter, but that on the far side, the wrong side, of the red line is something quite alien and other. That otherness, moreover, needs to be insisted upon, the declaration of its difference needs to be asserted. The pre-eminent fact about that inimical adjacent patch, that is blue, is that it is manifestly not green. "We are the Greens; do not confuse us with the Blues who live on the other side of the border and are not like us." Borders exist to keep green and blue apart and to remind everyone how important that separation is. The separation, the repudiation of blue, intensifies the special quality of the green, and those who protect its greenness from the contamination of the potentially invasive blue are the green's heroes and benefactors.

It is hardly surprising that for many who seek to cross them or are contained within them, borders are seen as racist.

So must there always be borders? What about the utopian idea that we are all one common humanity whatever physical space we occupy at a given moment? What happened to that benign, dreamily idealistic version of globalization?

Today I am in London in the depths of winter and the snow is falling. Routine in winter in the Welsh hills, snowfall in Bloomsbury is a rarity, but I decided to risk slithering along the pavements to pay a visit to the British Library. The uniform imposition of this white material on the roads and paving stones slows everyone down, softens the usual clamour, changes the atmosphere in ways that are rather pleasing. Normal routines have been gratifyingly subverted.

As I pass through the entrance arch of the Library the first thing I meet is Eduardo Paolozzi's great bronze statue of Isaac Newton, modelled on Blake's etching of the scientist bending down to take an important geometric measurement. On his broad curved back a delicate blanket of white snow has been laid. Born in Scotland to Italian immigrant parents, and interned in the Second World War as an enemy alien in his own country of birth, Paolozzi knew all about the purpose of borders. His father and grandfather, put on a ship to Canada while he himself was in prison in Scotland, drowned when a German U-boat hit their ship.

Picking my way across the British Library piazza, I push through the glass entrance doors and choose a quiet desk in the Reading Room. The weather has reduced numbers this morning.

I spread out on my desk a heap of books on "border theory" and "borderlands" and very quickly I am discovering the concept of "heterotopia", which border theorists have rather taken to. *Hétérotopie* was coined in the late 1960s by the French theorist Michel Foucault, to mean...well, who can be confident that he or she has understood Foucault? It seems to be a contrast to the idea of Utopia which means, literally, "no place", too impossibly perfect to exist in actuality. Heterotopias (literally, other places or different places, the term turning up in medicine to mean things being where they shouldn't) actually do exist, they are places where people go to be different, to be free, outside the dominant spaces they are officially supposed to inhabit. Delightfully, Foucault, having run through all sorts of categories and sub-categories of his idea, arrives at the ship, which he sees as the perfect example of heterotopia. It is "a floating piece of space, a place without a space, that exists by itself, that is closed in on itself and at the same time given over to the infinity of the sea". It has been for Western civilization, as well as the engine of commerce, "the greatest reserve of the imagination...In civilizations without boats, dreams dry up, (*les rêves se tarissent*) espionage takes the place of adventure, and the police take the place of pirates".

A floating entity like the ship, I take him to mean, is the ultimate repudiation of the idea that everything can be contained in one place, subject to border controls that are also controls over the mind, the imagination, and the spirit. Isn't it better to float in freedom on the ocean than have your papers asked for and a policeman demand where are you from and where are you going?

The problem with this dream of free-floating otherness is that it is not compatible with another, sharper kind of reality. It skids and crashes into the striped security barriers lowered by those for whom borders are attractive because they enclose spaces, define them, permit the fluttering of the tribal flag, mark out the sacred site, signal the privileged place. And that is not something that is confined to geographical borders. There are borders of the mind, of the sensibility, of culture, language, ethnicity, custom, of sheer *preference*. Far from wishing to see these dissolved, countless millions wish to see them preserved, strengthened, hardened, with more effective moats and defensive works put in place to repel the alien idea or feeling.

Whatever 'globalization' has done it has not resulted in a passion for melting down razor wire.

For the rest of the day I riffle through these pages, examine the catalogue, collect further tomes from the issue desk, find all sorts of interesting ideas and opinions, but somehow the essence of the thing is evading me. I decide eventually that what I am looking for is not here. It is time to return to the streets.

Outside, my eyes watchfully focussed on the slippery slush under my feet, I do not notice her at first. I look up at last and see that it is one of my former students and, after a bright enough greeting, I can see that actually all is not well. I ask what has upset her and out it all comes. Her teaching practice has not gone well. In a language exercise that matched words and pictures she used a picture of an amiable cartoon hound-dog with large floppy ears and a comical expression. Her Muslim students were outraged at the appearance of a filthy dog on the Powerpoint presentation. It is offensive, they shout, and the class erupts in chaos. She is distraught. The last thing she wanted to do was to cause offence.

But how does one know precisely when one has started to wander visa-less across the invisible borderlines of the mind?

2. Alligator Sneakers

I am in the passport queue at Heathrow Airport, having just disembarked from a plane from North Africa. I pick up the *Travelling to the UK* leaflet produced by the now abolished UK Border Agency and scan the neat slogan that summarises its mission statement: "Securing our border; controlling migration." The Border Agency knows where "our border" is and who "we" are. It understands the function of a border, deploys effortlessly its assured language of exclusion and inclusion. These people have the advantage of me. Not merely do they know where the border is, they want a border, and they want to police it. In the summer of 2013 the Government launched a poster campaign that shocked many people. Billboards, mounted on vans that were driven through areas of high immigration, shouted GO HOME OR FACE ARREST and blazoned the number of arrests for suspected illegal immigration the previous week in that area. A telephone number and a text message number were given for those who felt fearful. Even the xenophobic UK Independence Party branded the posters as "nasty". The next day it was revealed that the Government's immigration statistics were a shambles, little more than guesswork based on random surveys of samples of incoming passengers at airports. The public was baffled. Travel in and out of Britain requires such constant documentation and checks and computerised logging of personal data by airlines that no one could believe how the Government could claim that it did not know how many people were coming into the country. For the purposes of the immigration 'debate', an area of public discourse largely untouched by hard, measurable facts, this hardly mattered of course and the ritual exchange of prejudices went on as before.

Of course border officials have a job to do. As the leaflet explains, the Home Office is bound to intercept at the borders anything that belongs on the list of offensive weapons helpfully itemised in the leaflet: "flick and gravity knives, butterfly knives, push daggers, belt-buckle knives, death stars, swordsticks, stealth (non-metallic) knives, knives disguised as everyday objects, knuckledusters, blowpipes, truncheons and some martial arts equipment". Firearms, explosives and equipment, Samurai swords "with a curved blade exceeding 50cms in length" (which "can only be imported for an authorised purpose or function such as participation in martial arts events or religious ceremonies") are, one supposes, uncontroversial prohibitions. I imagine, too, that they are easily purchasable on arrival – with the possible exception of the blowpipe – if you have some violent or homicidal mission to accomplish during your stay.

But borders don't just keep out small weapons, pornography, endangered animals and plants, handbags made out of alligator skin, and rough diamonds, they keep out the wrong sort of people and the wrong sort of ideas. They keep in those they have no wish to see moving at liberty elsewhere. Borders have a lot of work to do. They matter especially to those who would control us and who would make us feel their power.

The queue today is long and slow. We shuffle along, feeling vaguely guilty, searching for some residue of transgression that can be dredged up. Was Gran Canaria really a duty-free zone? Should those seeds have been declared? Was it one litre of spirits plus one bottle of wine or two? We look suspiciously at those who have failed to sail through the entry-barrier, beneath that vast intimidating sign of relatively recent invention: UK BORDER written in giant letters. They are locked in dialogue with the border agents who are staring pitilessly into their computer screens where all truths are incontrovertible and all facts known. A passport photograph is examined with a *moue* of distaste We invent for them histories of malpractice. Terrorists, illegals, dodgy characters...And then the passport is handed back. They are waved through.

When it is my turn the agent inquires dryly: "Are you travelling alone, Sir?" I point across the aisle to my wife who is being processed at the neighbouring *guichet*. He looks unhappy at this answer but nods, curtly waves me through. Why did he ask me that? Do I look

like a paperless con-artist, a terrorist, a fake-passport holder, a
smuggler? Does he think I have a blowpipe stuffed in that small
backpack slung over my shoulder? A death star? A Samurai sword?
Alligator skin sneakers?

By now I am passing through the customs channel marked
Nothing to Declare. Should I have walked through the one that said
"European Union Citizens".Yes, I should have done, but who cares?
There is no one about. No one standing at those empty inspection
tables. Not even a single male traveller "of Middle-Eastern
appearance", as the news bulletins say, having his suitcase worked
over, its contents spread out untidily. There are no officials with
peaked hats like in the TV comedy sketches demanding that one
open the suitcase to reveal a dozen bottles of Scotch.

They are out of sight, watching us on camera. We live in a nation
of official voyeurs.

We go through the last barrier on to the shiny concourse. The
border has been crossed, we are Here and immediately lost in the
crowd, absorbed by anonymity, dispersed, untraceable, scattered.

3. No Nightmare on Main Street

I am in Morocco again, preparing to cross another border. Today's journey began in Casablanca, at the Hotel Excelsior. Built with some splendour in 1915 the Excelsior is now scuffed and faded. But I love these once grand old hotels that have lost their sheen. I like that way they have of clinging to a bare thread of old elegance that refuses to concede that they are in terminal decline. I still regret the disappearance of the Hotel Grande Bretagne on the harbour front at Lesbos with its brown painted wooden floors and spartan simplicity, now converted into a bank. So many of those old-fashioned Greek hotels have gone, unable to compete with the demand for mandatory *en suite* facilities, slick reception desks, flat screen TVs and Wifi. I have not been back either to Homer's "sandy Pylos" but I am sure that the quirky hotel I stayed in, *To Hypnos,* (Sleep) in that town will also have vanished.

Black and white cinema has ensured that everyone has a view about Casablanca. They know that it is a romantic place pulsing with mystery, glamour, intrigue but on the day of my visit the dominant impression is of dust and noise because the main street, Boulevard Mohamed V, has been torn up for the installation of a new tramway. This makes it more like the main street of a town in the Wild West. On either side of the road, crumbling Art Deco buildings seem poised in an uncertain state between demolition and refurbishment. Perhaps next time I come their modernist *chic* will have been restored. As I examine the handsome old flaking facades I wonder if this, too, is a kind of frontier, a perilous suspension between urban survival and inexorable, downwardly-spiralling decay, all touch and go, a fragile balance that could swing either way, like the British high streets with their boarded-up shopfronts, poised on the edge of collapse, hoping vainly for rescue rather than for the opening of another charity shop?

Before checking out from the hotel I spend some time in the Hotel Excelsior lobby examining the lovely floor and wall tiles, the fluted wooden pillars, the defunct but self-consciously preserved 1920s telephone switchboard. Quite soon I am noticed by the manager. He is wearing a smart suit and asks me where I am from. He is pleased at my admiration for the hotel's features and I sense that he is trying to stop its decline, perhaps dreaming of a major refurbishment, the restoration of its former glamour. But there are no foreign tourists staying as far as I can see. It is too scruffy and basic for the Trip Advisor crowd. But in my view it is clean where it matters, and, believe me, I have stayed in far, far worse. It would be invidious to name and shame but the Hotel Truva in Izmir...No, I won't say anything.

In a dark corner of the lobby two men sit smoking in a deep low sofa watching football on a large TV screen. They momentarily lift their eyes away from the game to examine me with inoffensive, curious smiles. They wave cigarettes in the air and I nod my head at them. Earlier, as I came down the gracious stairway, I had found that the whole of the first floor seemed to be closed down, access to the corridors denied by thick red plush curtains. In my room two formerly connected doors on either side suggested that a whole suite of rooms could have been booked, overlooking the clock tower and the old medina, a scurry of horses and carts and carriages where today the gridlocked traffic honks unceasingly, sounding its frustration at not being able to move.

I am leaving to catch the long distance bus to Tetouane this morning. It is a journey of a few hours and most Moroccan long distance buses these days are modern and comfortable. No pungent chickens escaping their boxes, and rank human scents like those that I recall from Morocco in the 1970s. I arrive in Tetouane in time for a haggle over a taxi that will take me to the border post that protects the second of my Spanish enclaves in North Africa, Ceuta. A boy in a yellow high-viz tabard steps forward to establish his authority. I am going to see a lot of these yellow vests, the equivalent of those peaked caps that self-appointed car park attendants in Italy used to wear back in the 1960s to justify putting their hands out for baksheesh. The boy, attaching himself to me without any encouragement, remains under the erroneous impression that he has guided me to the taxi rank which in fact I found by my own efforts as a result of striding a few paces. When I clamber into the taxi he pokes his head in and follows it by the delivery of an outstretched hand. I ignore it. He shrugs and moves off.

I am never easy with this feature of North African travel. Tourism so often strikes me as corrupting but its customs and practices are now too deeply entrenched for anything to change. It raises barriers, most obviously but not exclusively economic, between tourist and tout. It is the relationship of parasite to host body and who can say, in this feeding process, which is which? The racism (an unwillingness to respect the Other) can cut both ways and no one truly gains from these rites of mutual exploitation. It is not that one grudges anyone poorer than oneself a few pence (which is all that generally turns out to be required). It is more that one wants to go one's own way without molestation or abuse. Both of these, however, are too readily proffered and they demean both sides.

Once, in the Thai city of Chiang-Mai, a boy on a bicycle, clearly not a professional tout, pursued me for more than an hour. I genuinely think that he could not understand why anyone would want to wander serendipitously in a Thai city. "Where are you going?" he kept repeating plaintively. "Where are you going?" The fact that I neither knew nor cared where I was going, so long as I kept seeing interesting things, made no sense to him. I am sorry that he felt so troubled and could not trust me to go my own way.

I soon leave the boy in the yellow vest and start to concentrate on the taxi itself. It is battered and its engine clearly under strain. Even the driver struggles to close and wrench open the passenger doors. I am in doubt about whether it will even make it to the border but the driver is not bothered and he seems very happy and courteous. The journey of several miles costs next to nothing.

He pulls up at the frontier post and leaves me, with a nice smile, to find my way through the scatter of parked taxis, cars queuing to cross and small groups of people with the same goal. There are no signs, no information, so I just start walking. There is always something satisfying about walking across a border. It's not the same when you do it in a car or bus, or a night train immobile at the border post with the sound of strange voices and the dance of flashlights outside in the darkness.

Quickly I am besieged by touts who have got hold of supplies of the little white immigration *fiches* and it is clear what they will want from me for supplying them. I walk on. I try one of the *guichets* where someone is lurking in the dark interior. I hand over my passport and he shouts tetchily: "Paper! Paper!" Seeing that I don't have one of those *fiches*, he grudgingly hands out through his window a blank form and I fill it in. With the usual ill-grace of border officials he hands back the passport to me curtly after a long interval, the document having been given a hearty rubber stamp. I walk on to the Spanish line where a crowd of people is crushed against the narrow entrance to the passage through to Spanish territory.

Two Spanish policemen spot me and ask for my passport. I am quickly waved through, in contrast to the treatment given to the little knot of Moroccans. The burly policemen grab them roughly by the shoulder and fling them out of the way if they give the wrong answer to the query: "Residencia?".

I have seen farmers deal this way with recalcitrant sheep.

Once through the narrow space I am face to face with a giant hoarding welcoming me to Ceuta the "*ciudad de compras*", the town of shopping. Ceuta, like Melilla, is one of those anomalous survivals of the European imperial hold on Africa, another Spanish territory on the African coast. And of course it is also the ancient Abyla, forming in ancient history with Calpe (Gibraltar) the twin pillars of Hercules. Naturally, on the promenade in the centre of town there is a giant bronze of Hercules himself, parting the twin pillars and looking out to sea. The evening light is fading as I walk round the bay to find a hotel. This is palpably not Morocco. Everything changes so quickly when one crosses a border. One might have expected more gradual transitions. Ceuta is neat and tidy and very Spanish with its baroque Cathedral and marble flags. Later, I twiddle a sugar packet in the Bar Jota which tells me that Ceuta is the "*Perla del mediterraneo*". The town centre is unusually alive because the traditional eve of

Epiphany *cavalgades* or parades are just about to start. This proves to be a boisterous procession where, hemmed in at a fixed point by the crowds, I watch the costumed men, women and children walk past to celebrate their European Christian roots.

Next morning, however, I discover that there are quite a lot of Moroccans in Ceuta. That night I eat in a Moroccan restaurant. The waiter, out of courtesy rather than accuracy, compliments me on my French (the *lingua franca* in Morocco after Arabic and native dialects) which he says is not spoken much in Ceuta. Neither, I am to discover, is English. The waiter explains to me carefully that English people sometimes speak 'strangely', especially all those day trippers from Gibraltar. It is not, he points out with firm disapproval, 'normal English'. He then gives a very creditable imitation of the classic Cockney glottal stop: "Bo'lle of wa'er.". And, he adds, they are always saying: "Lovely jubbly."

The feast of the Epiphany or Three Kings begins in the morning with marching bands outside the Cathedral and lots of senior military men displaying a profusion of medals on their chests. In the church of Our Lady of Africa there is still a Christmas crib with a clothes line from which hang baby clothes, with more heaped in a basket near the manger. Presumably these are gifts from the faithful for poor mothers in the vicinity.

Next day I walk along the front and down to the ferry port to catch the late morning ferry from Ceuta to Algeciras in mainland Spain on the other side of the Straits of Gibraltar. There is not much in the way of security screening, the operator being lost in his sports paper while my bag trundles over the rollers of the conveyor belt, and anyway I am already in Spain, so why should anyone bother? As the ferry steams out I can see down on the quay the names "Pincho and Maria", plainly scribbled in the concrete when it was first wet and the words now set hard. Are Pincho and Maria still an item? These idle speculations are what travel is all about. On arrival at Algeciras, although my bag is actually put through screening once more, there are again no passport checks. I walk round the corner to the bus station where a bus is waiting for La Línea.

If the Spanish have to deal with the Moroccans' claim on Ceuta the British in turn have to think about the resentful Spanish claim on Gibraltar. On arrival at the bus station at La Línea there is, naturally, no mention of Gibraltar, no helpful direction signs, but, stepping out into the street, the looming Rock is a pretty unignorable guide (no one has any interest of course in making these crossings easier or better signposted).

I prepare to cross another frontier out of Spain into British territory. A graffiti artist has added the helpful information on the low wall of the border post that Gibraltar is "Fuck City". There is of course a passport official but he sits behind his counter with the placid immobility of a fish at the bottom of a deep pond and declines even to open my passport, waving me through with a minimal gesture of his head. This must be the most relaxed border I have ever strolled across.

And then it starts: the red phone box, the street-sign that says "Winston Churchill Avenue"... It is Saturday lunchtime – I have a gift for arriving at places at the wrong moment – and in Gibraltar everything, except the tawdriest of the tourist souks, shuts down at 2pm on Saturday until 9.am on Monday morning, by which time I will be preparing to leave. The dull weather, caused by a great dark cloud, the Levanter, that sits on top of the Rock, makes matters more gloomy. In sharp contrast to the cleanliness of Ceuta where you could eat your lunch off the main street, Gibraltar is surprisingly shabby and seedy, especially in the back streets. I board a bus in Winston Churchill Avenue but almost immediately it comes to a halt and stays motionless for more than fifteen minutes at a traffic light just inside the territory because it is the time of morning when the flights come in and out. It turns out that this airport runway (once a racecourse) is the first thing you cross when entering Gibraltar. It is like waiting at a rural level crossing for the train to go past. The lights change at last and I cross the wide flat strip of runway to the Rock itself. Not long after passing Morrison's supermarket I get off at Main Street and check in to the Cannon Hotel, a seedy B&B of a very familiar English stamp.

The Englishness of Gibraltar is of a slightly outdated kind. In the pubs, for example, like 'The Angry Friar' and the 'Horseshoe', plump, brash Mancunian barmaids practise the lost art of pulling a full pint measure of London Pride or John Smith's. One's hand sticks uncomfortably to the table tops, not cleaned since the last Royal Jubilee, people guffaw loudly from bar stools, and a film of blue fag smoke, from barmaid and customers, fills the pub. Naturally fish and chips are ubiquitous but also steak and kidney pie and everything that consorts naturally with chips and baked beans. Behind the bar of the 'Horseshoe', on Main Street, sailor's hats from HMS Endeavour, Ark Royal or Cumberland, signed by crew members, jostle with jokey pub signs ("Rules of the Management, No 1: The Boss is Always Right").

Next day I climb up to the Upper Rock where everything that is at all interesting on Gibraltar is to be found. I am relieved. It has been worth it after all. The natural underground caves, in mythology said to go down for ever or to be the conduit to Africa whence the Barbary apes originally came (presumably without *fiches*), have impressive stalactites and there are man made tunnels with dusty models of soldiers from the age of Trafalgar shouting: "Who Goes There?" when a light switch is tripped.

And, of course there are the apes — actually tail-less monkeys. Although one of them ran up and leapt on to me, clutching at my coat and refusing for some time to let go of my sleeve, they mostly keep their distance, perhaps sitting on a car roof, or on one of the innumerable cast iron cannon that appear at every turn. They have a strange delicacy, turning away shyly when one tries to photograph them.

On the last afternoon I walk out to Europa Point, the most southerly point of Europe. The shrine of Our Lady of Africa is naturally shut, it being a Sunday, and a giant mosque rather commandingly occupies a far larger amount of ground, looking towards Africa and nurturing the hope in Muslim hearts that the Moors will return to claim their ancient territory of Al-Andalus. No doubt it is closed on Fridays.

I am not sure I am looking for a symbol but I find it in the failing light. A garage door is open under some retirement flats looking out over the Strait. An elderly, red-faced Englishman in a cravat is bending over with some difficulty and breathing heavily. With an oily rag he is cleaning the spokes of his bicycle.

4. The Inn-Keeper of Europe

J'ai été pendant quatorze ans l'aubergiste de l'Europe – Voltaire

It is my first taste of tear-gas and my eyes are streaming, even at this distance from the centre of the police action. This is not what I expected from my first visit to the decorous Protestant city of Geneva.

I did not, it is true, expect to like a place generally taken to be devoted to money, a subject which holds little interest for me except on those reasonably frequent occasions when I do not have enough of it. My eye mists over when I pass a shop-window of fabulously expensive come-mug-me gold watches, heavy with the absurdity and pomp of Philistine display. And here in Switzerland was where Nazi gold, or contemporary funds embezzled by dictators of various stripes from aid agencies or the public coffers of their people, lay in anonymous vaults reached through numbered accounts.

But from the outset I was intrigued, charmed, fascinated by this city on a lake behind which in the distance the peak of Mont Blanc glittered in the cold winter light.

It was my luck to be at the bus-stop outside the central railway station, the Gare Cornavin, where buses leave for Ferney-Voltaire in the French province of Gex, a short hop across the Swiss border, during a demonstration that looked peaceful enough to me but which the massed police decided was not, spraying clouds of tear-gas – with little regard to the rest of us – across the entrance to the station and forcing everyone to run inside, handkerchiefs over our mouths.

This international centre of finance and global humanitarian organisations, which has the paradoxical air of a small provincial city, may not seem like the natural site of public disorder (though later I was told that demonstrations are actually quite frequent) but a move to ban the construction of minarets on good Protestant soil was being proposed by the Genevan authorities and this was the trigger on this day for the protestors.

In this punctilious bourgeois town there is no flyposting or graffiti so instead I went to inspect the political posters on billboards provided for the purpose outside the town hall. "*Pas de nouvelle guerre de religion en Suisse*, one poster declared. "*Repartir en croisade?*" [Are we off on another crusade?] asked another.

John Calvin's city already has a synagogue, a Russian Orthodox cathedral with glorious gilt onion domes, even an English church, but the move against minaret-building reflected the new fear in Europe of Islamism and the mood was animated. I would come to the city again, one mid-December on the night of the celebrations of *L'Escalade*. This is the opportunity for the white middle class citizens of Geneva (I merely record the evidence of my eyes) to dress up in historical costume and parade through the streets to mark the great event of 1602 when another monstrous theocratic threat, Catholicism, was seen off. On the night of 11 December, when the troops of the Duke of Savoy craftily made an attempt to scale the city walls on a ladder (*l'escalade*) they had a pan of scalding soup tipped on their heads by one Catherine Cheynel, a mother of 14, whose watchful action roused the town, with the happy result that the vile papists were repulsed. The *fête* I witnessed was a jolly enough affair, though very decorous and Genevois, with lots of plastic cups of mulled wine and well-behaved vivacity in the streets.

Before I arrived in Ferney-Voltaire I had mistakenly assumed that it was actually on the Swiss side of the border, chosen by the controversial *philosophe* as a refuge from the French authorities. The truth turns out to be far more complex and in a sense rather puzzling. Ferney, when the sexagenarian philosopher arrived in 1758, was a French hamlet but today it is a sizeable little town in what the local tourist office now calls the *pays de Voltaire*. "Come and cultivate your garden in Voltaire country, a stone's throw from Geneva," they propose, alluding to one of those famous phrases (like *pour encourager les autres*) that we all remember from Voltaire's satirical masterpiece *Candide*. Written in the wake of the terrible 1755 Lisbon earthquake that shook the confidence of the Enlightenment about its prescriptions for the growth of human happiness through the application of reason, *Candide* tilted at the supposedly facile optimism of Leibniz and was, and remains, a huge success. It is probably the only work of Voltaire that most people have read. In his day, however, he was principally celebrated as a playwright, seeming even to eclipse the reputation of Corneille and Racine, though his plays are no longer performed or read except by scholars. Voltaire's classical verse tragedies – he abhorred the wayward genius of Shakespeare with his low life characters, refusal to abide by the classical unities, and wholly undignified diction – were actually reaching the end of their shelf-life in his own time, in spite of their contemporary success with Parisian audiences at the Comédie Française where his statue still dominates one of the foyers.

Cultivating his garden, it turns out, is exactly what the author did on his estate at Ferney, planting orchards and turning himself into a landed gentleman and benefactor, which is how he is celebrated today in Ferney-Voltaire (as it became) where there are no fewer than two Voltaire statues in the streets of this pleasant but bland little town. One monument celebrates him as "The Benefactor of Ferney", which he certainly was. The citation on the stone plinth records that he had a hundred houses built, presented the town with a school, hospital, reservoir and fountain, handed out interest free loans to the local community, drained the marshes, established fairs and local markets, and fed the inhabitants during the 1771 famine. The other plinth calls him simply the *Patriarche de Ferney*. As Ian Davidson's lively biography of the Ferney years, *Voltaire in Exile*, shows, Voltaire's earlier career hardly pointed to the public-spiritedness of his later period. He spent most of his life in vigorous pursuit of the rich and famous – even as he relished provoking and satirising them. The establishment gadfly is a phenomenon we have grown used to – one thinks of Christopher Hitchens, 'the Great Contrarian' who could hardly have been said to have been ostracised in his lifetime or to have lived under a cloud of obscurity – and Voltaire had friends and enemies in equal number at court. He was also a very rich man, not just from his successful plays, but from his financial dealings that enabled him to buy properties, lavishly rebuild them, and spread his wealth around to others.

Voltaire arrived in Switzerland in 1755 from Prussia where he had been at Potsdam at the court of Frederick the Great as Chamberlain and poet-in-residence until he fell out with the King in a pamphlet war and was sent packing. In France it seems to have been held against him that he had preferred to live with the Prussian King and when he came back to France Louis XV banned him from Paris and Versailles (for reasons, however, that are still not wholly clear and that continue to perplex his biographers) and this is why he fetched up in Switzerland initially and then in the French town of Ferney. He started in Geneva (then an independent republic that was not part of the Swiss Federation) because his bankers, doctors, and printers (all of interest to the 60-year-old poet and financial speculator) were there. He acquired a property he called "Les Délices" and moved between it and another at Lausanne where the winter climate was better and then in 1758 he arrived at Ferney, acquiring also an estate at nearby Tournay. Not previously known for any interest in the fate of ordinary people as opposed to courtiers, he became aware of the poor state of the hamlet and its rural economy and proceeded to do his bit to regenerate it. He also became interested in penal reform, prompted by several notorious cases that illustrated the corrupt and barbarous nature of eighteenth century French criminal justice and its (literally, one might think) unholy relationship with the Catholic church of which, in spite of all his barbs, he remained a member until his death when the church and his fellow *philosophes* quarrelled over his corpse. He became actively involved in several high-profile cases of wrongful execution and used his influence to rectify wrongs and gain compensation for the victims' families, and wrote pamphlets about them.

Voltaire also lived, not without occasional strain, with his niece, Marie-Louise Denis, and she was probably responsible for the creation at the chateau of Ferney of a lively social scene which turned it into a stopping place on the Grand Tour for so many young writers, like the youthful James Boswell who left a vivid sketch of Voltaire. The latter described himself sardonically as "the inn-keeper of Europe", ruefully counting up the number of visitors he was forced to entertain.

But it was the theatre that was at the centre of Voltaire's life and he built several at Ferney, and in the neighbourhood, putting on performances of his own plays in which he himself often acted. That was until he found that he was not even in a fit state to play an old man as he entered his seventies in increasingly ill-health and pain from the prostate cancer that eventually killed him. The theatre, of course, was anathema to the Calvinists which is why he could never have lived permanently in Geneva, the tiny (or *parvulissime* as he called it) republic whose pastors sometimes covertly came to his theatrical performances. Geneva did not like Voltaire, who had written disparagingly about the place in his Genève entry for the *Encyclopédie* and who had taken up the cause of the city's downtrodden lower classes. Geneva was a society rigidly stratified into four classes and at the top they enjoyed an extraordinary autocratic power exercised by the *Petit Conseil* which seemed a law unto itself. Voltaire backed the *natifs* at the bottom of the pile and when they were forced to seek exile after their demands were rebuffed by the oligarchs he had the bright idea of establishing across the border at Ferney a watch-making industry, using their talents in that trade. It turned out to be a great financial success.

I walked out to the chateau which, with my luck, was closed at this season. I peered through the locked iron gates like a peasant of the *ancien régime*, dazzled by the splendid living of my betters, then I crunched back through the leaves and autumnal mud to catch my bus back to Geneva.

As I later walked the streets of the city, where I had been commissioned by a national newspaper to write a travel feature on "48 Hours in Geneva" (which necessitated a conscientious tramp around all its streets and sights) I still thought about Ferney. I struggled yet again to make sense of the world of frontiers and borders. The bus from Ferney whizzes across the border without stopping. The frontier posts seem merely perfunctory and this, one feels, is how it should be – in the best of all possible worlds.

On Saturday mornings Genevans flock across by car or with their shopping trolleys on the bus to Ferney for its stunning open air market. The "farmer's markets" one sees in English towns cannot be mentioned in the same breath as this awesome display. The riches of the produce (and I was there on a cold late November morning well out of any growing season) were overwhelming. One stall sold nothing but oysters of every size, shape and variety. Another had only salad leaves in equal profusion. Another bread, another olives, others similarly exclusive for olive oil, wine, fruit, cheese, fish, game including unskinned rabbits and pheasant, sausages, pâté. Then there were prepared meals from the *traiteur* of every kind including many varieties of pasta, roast chicken on spits, even roast halal chickens, all stretching along the length of the town centre. No doubt there was equal traffic of Ferneyites in the opposite direction, for example to the extensive flea market at the Plainpalais in Geneva where every kind of junk and antique was spread out on the ground or on trestle tables. This interchange, but also this variety, the knowledge that on the other side of the border there may be something different or better, is a compensation of sorts for having frontiers. It can be – and now at last I have found a positive aspect of the border – a *promise* of difference, seen not as a badge of exclusion, but rather an invitation to share in what is not immediately ours by custom or right or local entitlement. The border crossing, in this light, opens up a tempting prospect of discovery and the thrill of true diversity. It proposes a celebration of the cherished fact that we do not all do things in the same way, dress in the same clothes, eat the same food, or dissolve our unique traits in the globalised soup.

At the most difficult time for Voltaire in his Ferney period, in 1765 when the public executioner in Paris burnt his *Dictionnaire Philosophique Portatif*, and he feared for his own safety, the writer dreamed of a utopian community of like-minded *philosophes* and approached Denis Diderot to sound him out. But where did he propose to locate this utopia? In border country of course. At Clèves, or Kleve as it is now, on the border between Germany and the Netherlands. Voltaire pleaded with Diderot: "A man like you must only see with horror the country in which you have the misfortune to live. You should come to a country where you would have complete liberty, not only to print whatever you want, but to preach out loud against superstitions that are as infamous as they are blood-stained...You could establish a Chair which would be the Chair of Truth."

Of all the impossible frontiers to cross, the one which divides the real world from Utopia is the most strongly fortified and possesses the fiercest and most obdurate passport officials. The Chair of Truth would have struggled to find a satisfactory incumbent.

The first posthumous edition of Voltaire's works, edited by the philosopher Condorcet, was known as the Kehl edition because that is where it was published, across the Rhine from Strasbourg and therefore just out of reach of the French authorities. Voltaire, notwithstanding all those Parisian monuments and statues and squares named after him, was a man who belonged at the edge, ready to scurry if necessary across the nearest border – to Somewhere Else.

5. Transbalkan

Even the most interesting and adventurous journey can begin in a wholly unglamorous way. This was the substance of Paul Theroux's argument with his fellow travel writer Bruce Chatwin: that the latter never told you enough about the practical details of the journey, of what means were actually employed to connect A with B. To prove his point, Theroux begins *The Old Patagonian Express* with a description of catching the subway from his home in Boston. Fans of Chatwin – who famously hated being called a travel writer – would dismiss this as being beside the point. You read him for the magic of his prose, they would say, and, like the other problem that he may have fibbed a bit, what matters is the glamour of the story. Don't bring us down to earth. Don't rub our noses in the banal.

There is nothing stylish or Chatwinesque about a London night bus at four in the morning in Theobalds Road. The N8 was packed with people, a few of them apparently sober, whooping and shouting, calling friends on mobiles, fixing up to meet in the pub later that day, enjoying a shared party atmosphere. The din prevented any private conversation. I got off at Liverpool Street and caught the train to Stansted airport where a good breakfast at Ponti's of sausage and scrambled egg started to make me human again. Even the lifeless language of airports ("cars left unattended will be subject to a tow-away procedure") seemed less obnoxious with a good cup of coffee and breakfast tucked away. And there was the excitement to come of six borders to cross in the next couple of weeks.

The early plane touched down at Prague airport a few hours later. I had a reason to be in the city again. I was writing a biography of Franz Kafka and I wanted to pace the streets a little, for this most strange and fabulating modernist was also a writer deeply rooted in his native city. "Kafka was Prague and Prague was Kafka," a Czech critic famously said and the local tourist industry wouldn't dissent from that, even if Kafka's official place in Czech culture (he wrote in German when the country was under the control of the Austro-Hungarian Empire) is still not completely secure.

I started next morning by walking all the way to the new Jewish Cemetery at Strašnice, only to find it was shut for a Jewish holiday. So I got a tram back to the city centre where my wife and I had coffee with a friend, Mrs Treterová, in the famous Cafe Slavia. She had returned from years in the United States and was enjoying being back in her birthplace again, liberated from fast food and fast living. In Prague, she insisted, "They know how to enjoy life". She praised the quiet, the leafiness, the trams. I am sorry that she had only a few years of this retirement in her civilised birthplace before she died.

A return to the Jewish cemetery and the distinctive modernist gravestone of Kafka, would have to wait for another trip, in the depth of winter, one I describe in the opening pages of my biography:

> At the gates of the New Jewish Cemetery in the Prague suburb of Strašnice, a lean and ancient custodian emerges to greet the visitor. He gestures towards a cardboard box, set on a small chair, from which one is invited to select a paper yarmulke, or skull-cap. With a dry smile, he accepts, on this bitterly cold February morning, the substitute of a woolly hat. Over his shoulder, it is impossible to miss a spotted white enamel sign, which reads, above a slender black arrow, DR FRANZ KAFKA.
>
> It was another such dull day – in spite of the date – in the late afternoon of 11 June 1924, when the doctor of law was buried here, among the dark, ornate gravestones of the Prague Jewish bourgeoisie. Coming upon the grave at the end of a gravel path, one is immediately struck by its difference: a grey, tapering, Cubist lozenge on which are printed the names of Kafka and the parents he preceded to the grave. In its formal simplicity, its shapely lightness, its unobtrusive but wholly original presence, it could not be more fitting as a memorial to a writer whose unique genius continues to fascinate the world and to baffle its attempts at interpretation.

But for now we were anxious to get on, and next day, after breakfast of turkish coffee (*turecka*) and doughnut in the splendid but scruffy Kavarna Fantova, in the old Prague station booking hall, named after Josef Fanta the architect – and where the international clocks around the wall were having their typically Czech joke by showing completely the wrong time – we caught the 8.58 Bratislava train. It was on time and very clean and spacious with good large windows. At first it bowled along through very flat country, then the landscape became more wooded and mountainous. At Brno, platoons of businessmen prowled the platform and a group of noisy wine salesmen climbed aboard.

We soon reached our first border crossing into Slovakia at Breclav where a swarm of passport officials buzzed on to the train. The first check was carried out by a Czech official but he was followed a few minutes later by a much meaner-looking Slovakian with a fierce moustache, a large rubber stamp, and that truculent, suspicious, faintly outraged demeanour of the true frontier official. How dare anyone think that they can just cross from one country to another? Just like that! Who do you take us for? And why do you want to enter my country anyway? Why should I grant you the privilege? What will you do here? If I had my way people like you would never be allowed beyond this point.

But of course the train, after a long pause, was allowed to slouch forward towards the Slovakian capital, Bratislava. We arrived at lunchtime and caught a tram from the station as far as the Danube where we started to search for a hotel. They all seemed full and we were eventually directed to one of the "botels" moored on the river bank. The cabin was comfortable enough and the humid smell of the Danube drifted in through the open window. All night we listened to the gentle throb of dredgers and other river traffic, forgetting that a mild evening by the water also means waking to a rash of mosquito bites.

After a day's exploration of the capital we set off next morning for border No 3, between Slovakia and Hungary. At Rajka the almost empty train was boarded by three frontier officials made up from both countries all of whom seemed to be working well enough in concert. It was one of those old-fashioned corridor trains and the three of them, on arrival at our compartment, with a noisy clatter of boots, drew back the door and entered with a flourish. The last of them, a Hungarian, had the very special privilege and pleasure of wielding the rubber stamp.

When they had finished with us the train slowly edged on towards the suburbs of Budapest. We would enjoy exploring the city, its dramatically split site, and its grand buildings, but were impatient to move on. Late the next evening, we walked into the central station to board our train to Sofia, capital of Bulgaria.

We had booked the Transbalkan Express in London but weren't entirely sure what to expect. I walked warily along the platform of a long, eighteen-coach train that looked as though it had been stitched together out of oddments. Each coach was a different colour, design and condition as if it had been borrowed or stolen from some international railway siding where abandoned rolling stock was left to die. There was an inescapable mystery. Who actually was in charge of this train and of putting it together? Did these assorted company liveries mean anything or had each compartment long ago been decommissioned? Who owned the parts of this peculiar train? Would anyone claim responsibility for its eventual passage? I passed a rather disconsolate German backpacker who said plaintively: "I want to go to Istanbul." The train was labelled "Transbalkan" and was due to terminate at Saloniki in Greece. The scruffiest coach of all was No 13 and it seemed that we were going to be its sole occupants all the way to Sofia. The sleepy Bulgarian guard who was responsible for coach 13 roused himself from his little cabin where he had been heating some coffee on a ring, possibly hoping that there would be no passengers at all. He smiled and quickly introduced us to what seemed at first to be his only two words of English: "I am conductor" and "toilet". I shudder to recall that last facility.

We had been wise enough to predict that there would be no dining car and, once the train had moved off into a darkness brightened by a large full moon, we began to unpack a picnic of food we had bought at the Smatch supermarket in the centre of Budapest. The feast consisted of wine, cheese, bread, tomato, and a tin of lentil and sausage. We had the compartment to ourselves, indeed the whole coach, and through the windows, as we slowed at local stations, a strong waft of hay, dung, and farm animals, entered in. We had finished eating by the time we hit border crossing No 4 – or was it 4a? – at Lokoshaza and a fierce blonde in camouflage uniform came stomping down the corridor and wrenched open the sliding door of the compartment. With that attitude of impatient distaste for anyone trying to cross a border to which we had now grown accustomed she snatched the passports, inspected them, then handed them back gracelessly. She then demanded of the cringing conductor that he unlock every single one of the locked carriages even though they were patently empty.

It was dark and we were confused about where we were. We may still have been in Hungary but the Romanian border was obviously close. Or was this it? The train remained motionless for more than an hour and a half. Dogs barked in the night. There were occasional shouts. Then at midnight the train lurched forward slowly – only to hiss to a halt again several minutes later at Vama which we could see was in Romania because the national flag was planted all along the platform.

Here a new set of officials came thumping along the corridor.

"Tourists?" the man in uniform asked.

We nodded and he wrote our names on a scrap of paper, dragged the door back to the closed position, and left. Once again there was silence and stillness broken only by an occasional outbreak of voices. After half an hour we felt the train starting to move forward slowly. We were on our way and as it was now nearly one in the morning we prepared to climb into our bunks, but scarcely had we got under the sheets when there was another rap on the door. This time it was two men in blue railway uniforms with peaked caps. One was tall, thin and silent. The other was small and plump and cheerful but his smiling demeanour contained a threat. He examined our tickets and shook his head sadly.

"No good," he said firmly.

"What?"

"No good. Ticket no good."

"What do you mean, 'no good'?"

"No good. Ticket no good."

"But these are perfectly legitimate international railway tickets. Look at them."

He smiled happily.

"No good. Ticket no good."

He pulled out from his pocket a sketchy railway map and started on a long rigmarole about the fact that the route the train was taking was 107 kilometres longer than the route we had paid for. This was obvious nonsense as an international train, passing through several countries is an international train and the rate is the international rate agreed by the railway authorities. But this was our first major mistake, to engage in reasoned debate. We should have understood that reason was beside the point. If you are a Romanian railway official it is considered a legitimate perk of the job to supplement your wages in this way. When I later complained to Rail Europe at their London office on my return they said without surprise: "Oh, yes, we know all about that."

Having just undressed and got into bed we were unwilling to get into an argument nor did we see any reason to compromise and I said flatly that I was not paying any bogus 'supplement'. The little fat man changed his mood abruptly.

"Passport!" he demanded sharply

"I am not surrendering my passport to a ticket inspector," I said with as pompous an air as I could manage.

He then threatened to put us off the train at the next stop. But all the time the threats were delivered in a relaxed way, as if we all understood that this was just a game and that all we had to do was to enter into the spirit of it. Why were we insisting on making such a fuss? Just hand over the money. *That's what everyone else does.* It is the way of the world. We can't fathom why you are wasting energy like this.

With a confident smile, knowing that they would be back and that their prey had nowhere else to go, they got up and left the compartment. We heard their raised voices, berating the conductor who had been hovering outside. Then, as a sort of reprise, they hammered on the door again but this time we decided to ignore them, having taken the precaution of locking the door from the inside.

When we woke the next morning in the grey dawn light we started to look out of the window. We felt as though we had been drawn back into the middle of the previous century. At small stations people stood patiently with their bundles and in the fields the poor peasants bent down at their toil as if in a painting by Courbet. Along a bridleway at right angles to the train a horse drawn cart raced towards us, raising a cloud of dust.

We found that it was just about possible to wash in cold water in a deep sink hidden under a table in the corner. Above it there was an empty cupboard with a shaving socket, taped over. None of the reading lights worked.

At 8.30 there was a hammering on the door. We knew who it would be and promptly let them in, as if they were a pair of cats returning home after a night's foraging. They seemed refreshed and happy, ready to start on us again. After all, what else did they have to do to occupy them? We resumed the argy-bargy but it rapidly became clear that they were impervious to any argument. We had now reached the point that we should have attained the previous night. Quick and total capitulation was all that had ever been required. Accordingly, I took out my wallet and produced a British £10 note. They exchanged smiles and looked at us tolerantly, like indulgent parents prepared to overlook a naive infraction. The plump little hand reached out and snatched the banknote with a friendly smile. There was of course no attempt at issuing an excess ticket, at estimating what 107 extra kilometres would have cost. I asked for a receipt and both the men laughed out loud at the absurdity of this. These foreigners certainly have a sense of humour, their exchanged glances seemed to say. But eventually seeing I was serious, the little man pulled out from his official pocket-book a scrap of paper and grandly wrote me out a 'receipt'. The two officials were now both wreathed in smiles, happy that we had seen sense at last. The one who had been doing all the talking trousered the banknote with a contented slap of his thigh.

I resumed my act of pompous outrage and said that I would make an official complaint to the Romanian embassy when I returned to London. They both laughed out loud at this. Crazy foreigners who think there is any official accountability or court of appeal in any country. He shrugged his shoulders and looked across at his silent partner:

"Government no good."

The Romanians, he added, as if to underline the impossible might of bureaucracy against which the little man must direct his puny and ultimately futile efforts, were ruled from Austria. Not since 1918, I reflected, but by now all we wanted was to see the back of them rather than engage in a history lesson and we bade farewell, everyone smiling and happy at a good job well done.

Later, as the train came to a halt for half an hour at the central station at Bucharest, I saw the two officials walk past our window, laughing and animated, celebrating the providential gift of what was probably a week's or even a month's wages. Our Bulgarian conductor, whose name was Atonas and who sympathised with us after they had gone, shrugged his shoulders and observed tartly:

"*Roman!*"

I take this to translate as: "What do you expect of a Romanian in an official uniform?"

It was by now time for another border crossing, No 5, at Giurgiu where the Bulgarian customs officers boarded the train, determined to do a thorough job. They stormed through the empty carriage, removing roof panels and wriggling through to see if any contraband or illegals were hidden there. When they had finished rattling and crashing and shouting the train started moving again, slowly inching along the Friendship Bridge over the Danube, built in 1954 when a Stalinist compact of 'friendship' united the two countries. Atonas suddenly burst into the carriage and slammed the windows shut. He pointed to a foul Romanian chemical plant that he clearly considered toxic. Just about to enter his own country again, he was becoming more patriotic. Half an hour before arrival at Sofia he would emerge from his cubicle in a smart official suit.

At Russe we had a final passport check and arrived at Sofia just before midnight. The station was bleak, unlit, the escalators did not function, and outside most of the street lights were out. But we were glad to leave our shabby temporary home and check into a dingy, allegedly three-star, hotel, 'The Sun', near the station and collapse into sleep.

Next morning we looked out of the window and saw a row of women opposite selling flowers from buckets and holding up a bunch in each hand. Then a man with a violin and a lumbering dirty grey bear at the end of a chain came past, the bear's fur was the colour of the carpet in coach 13. In spite of anxious warnings from the hotel staff about pickpockets we enjoyed Sofia. In the City Garden men were very seriously playing open-air chess with clocks, the sets rented out for use on the park benches. Fountains played and, as in the public spaces of Budapest, large numbers of people were reading in absorbed silence.

We took a trip out to the National Museum of History but were warned by the hotel that we could easily miss our stop on the bus:

"Because it was formerly the headquarters of the Communist Party it was hidden behind trees."

It certainly was a monstrosity – giant and ugly with marble floors and walls, glass chandeliers, carved wooden panels and brutalist mosaics. The historical display was a bit of a jumble and the famous Thracian gold turned out to consist of replicas. When I got back to the hotel I saw that my day rucksack had been slashed with a razor blade and then I remembered someone brushing against me in the street. Nothing was taken, however, my valuables having been stowed in a less exposed place.

When we left the next day at midnight from Sofia central railway station we found a much cleaner coach and a brisk, efficient steward who handed us fresh towels and soap. We were heading for Saloniki in northern Greece and, at four o'clock in the morning, we arrived at our final border post, No 6, at Kaleta. Bulgarian officials rounded up all the passports and took them away, presumably to an office on the station for computer checks. We were nervous. Where had they taken them? When would we get them back? *Would* we get them back? Nearly an hour later, however, they returned with the passports and, yet again, the train lurched slowly forward. After five minutes, however, it slumped to a halt again at Promohon Hellas on the Greek side. Not to be outdone, the Greeks now rounded up all the passports and took them away. They were returned an hour later and we moved off.

Three hours later we would arrive at Saloniki. We clambered off the train, deciding that six border crossings were more than enough for one trip. On the other side of the street from the railway station was a little cafe serving Greek coffee in tiny white cups, its tables splashed with morning sun. We sat down, stretched, soaked up the warmth and looked forward to a day of old-fashioned walking in the freedom of the city.

We had had our fill of borders.

6. The Last Frontier

I am driving through the Forest of Dean, that part of Gloucestershire that has always seemed to me to be a special place, a law unto itself, hosting a large working class community (famously depicted by the playwright Dennis Potter) in a very English county parts of which are very decidedly rich and patrician.

Not all inhabitants of the Forest were created equal; boundaries are very much to the point here. For example, if you were born within the boundary of the hundred of St Briavels you can call yourself a true Forester. Within this category you may, provided that you are an adult male, and have worked for a year and a day in one of the area's coal or iron mines, acquire a further status as a freeminer, with a right to extract coal or ore from common land, a right that survived even the nationalisation of the coal industry in 1946. In October 2010 this discriminatory provision was successfully challenged by Elaine Morman who qualified in all other respects except gender. The Forestry Commission was forced to back down and allow her to be a freeminer. Over a hundred of these operate today in the Forest of Dean.

But these are not the thoughts that pre-occupy me as I drive through the dappled light of a crisp April day in the Forest. I am thinking of another kind of boundary, older even than these ancient demarcations with their associated rights. It is as old as life itself. I am of course referring to death.

Although there are parts of the world where the border will never be crossed by those on either side of it, most borders turn out to be crossable for most people most of the time. Especially when it is a case of the hated neighbour performing the useful tasks of the *gastarbeiter*, tasks that no one on the favoured side of the border wants to dirty their hands with. But the frontier on my mind today has a checkpoint that only those who claim to have had 'near-death experiences' will have had any sort of inkling of.

Though most world religions have a view about what is on 'the other side' it remains, as Shakespeare pointed out in *Hamlet*, the bourn from which no traveller returns. We have no eyewitness accounts, only the vivid terrors painted by the mediaeval artists of northern Europe who wanted to show us what the other side would turn out to be like, especially for the unshriven and godless. In our peaceable Western suburbs where war has not been seen for some time (having become something that happens on TV in faraway hot places) the Hells of Hieronymous Bosch or Brueghel remain vivid metaphors and ones that must have terrified the plain people of their day – which was presumably their intention. Horrible, violent deaths still occur, even here, far from the war zones, but for most of us the queue for that last visa will move at a slower, more orderly pace.

It is never – how could it be? – comfortable to watch someone make the approach to death. Or grow old and infirm.

I turn off the leafy road now into the grounds of a large building with featureless glass and concrete annexes added to the original Victorian mansion in recent decades. There are benches set here and there on the lawns but they are empty. A picnic table is still in winter quarantine. Small seas of daffodil nod in the breeze, their yellow trumpets tossing back the fresh sunlight. Through the glass windows I can see the familiar sight of high-backed chairs set around the wall of the residents' lounge. Once inside I see the group of elderly people at closer quarters, staring out into the empty space between them as if they have been obliged to participate, with whatever degree of reluctance, in some Christmas parlour game.

I want to be distracted from all this and so I start to follow that thought. In my Liverpool childhood in the 1950s those games were still played. It was a world before games withdrew into a more private sphere in which even the communal TV screen was to give place to the individual flickering hand-held small screens of smart phones and tablet computers on slumped, overfed Christmas afternoons. There would still have been a piano in the living room on which an aunt with the right kind of facility would play the music for pass-the-parcel, stopping abruptly at random moments so that another layer of paper could be torn off the parcel before she started up again. During the 1960s those stolid upright pianos all vanished. Where did they go?

One of our games was called Family Coach. Each of us was assigned a part (the wheel, the picnic basket, the rear door, the front door, you get the idea) and someone (usually my father) was appointed the narrator of the coach's journey. Which of us, in 1950s north Liverpool, had ever seen a coach outside the museum stables of a stately home? If my father described the wheel falling off on a steep corner then whomsoever was the wheel was required to stand up and perform a 180 degree rotation (twice, I think). As I say, you get the idea, and you are already feeling sorry for us. It sounds like the sort of warming-up exercise that very expensive executive training courses would put their clients through on the soft carpets of some plush country hotel. As a way of getting people animated and laughing and interacting with each other, however, it certainly worked.

No one is laughing in this public parlour in the heart of the Forest of Dean. In the corner of the large lounge an ancient skinny woman keeps shouting at regularly-paced intervals: "Shit!", "Shit!" On a subsequent visit it will gradually dawn on me that her teeth don't fit and what she is saying is: "Six!" "Six!". Six what I never did find out. Six children who never came to visit? Six years of marriage before he disappeared? Six months incarcerated in this place?

The person we have come to visit is not mad or jabbering but the wisdom of 'elderly care' means that everyone over a certain age is tossed into this pit regardless of the nature of their affliction. A temporary physical problem following surgery means, for someone over the age of sixty five, being penned in a room with a group of men and women (though mostly the latter) some of whom are mad or demented. It means the eternal, booming, unwatched TV up on a bracket jutting from the wall. It means meals with unappetising smells. It means encountering a seemingly normal elderly man in the dining-room who suddenly threatens violence and has to be escorted away by the care staff. It means hours of being motionless in those tall vinyl thrones while the trees in spring leaf thrash outside in the wind.

It means denial of the dignity of silence and solitude, of decent human peace.

I watched her later decline (accelerated by this first sequestering?) and then came to her final resting place in a solicitous 'home', a good and caring place in an English cathedral city. She had been sent there shortly after surviving a false alarm on a bleak Sunday afternoon in that leafy 'home' in the Forest of Dean that had brought the family to her bedside. An over-zealous foreign locum doctor buzzed impatiently with a form to be signed, to cover his back, to give consent to non-resuscitation. In case. But the patient, on what the professionals call the 'care pathway', lingered for nearly a year in the new place, cut off from our world, unable to speak or acknowledge her children and friends, in the fathomless silent place granted to her by a paralyzing body dementia, fed by a drip, motionless, like someone in a perpetual sleep.

The poets have, unsurprisingly, been fond of the metaphor of sleep to represent the idea of death, the pale silence of the inert dreaming body seeming to prefigure its final going to rest and dreamless sleep. That border between death and life, brutally real in its immediate manifestation, in the terrible clarity of grief and loss, is at the same time less clearly marked in the longer perspective. The dead continue to visit us, in memory or in imagined hauntings. There is a vast literature of the supernatural but even the determinedly rational mind knows that death is not the end, that we recall, revisit, make dialogues with the dead, hearing their voices, feeling their influence, even obeying, posthumously, their commands.

One day I open the wardrobe, in the small room that is decorated by some of her own paintings, and I see row upon row of those bottles of liquid feed that the nurses will regularly change, briskly and breezily hooking up the new replacement.

Will I ever again see anything quite so bleak and desolate?

Silently, I ask myself: will no one come to lift the barrier and let her through?

7. Pudding Island

I am on a train on a journey that will ultimately take me to Wales – a country that has traditionally been held at arm's length by those Foresters of Dean in spite of the Welsh border lying only a few miles away from them – but for now I am moving slowly through the Cotswolds, the richer side of Gloucestershire with its yellow stone, old spires, and expensive cars packed like tinned fish in the station car parks at Kingham and Charlbury where commuters to London (travelling there for business or for stiff-and-shiny-carrier-bag designer shopping) have left them for the day.

That larger than life and idiosyncratic Victorian traveller, Sir Richard Burton, once observed: "England is the only country where I never feel at home." At the age of nine he was uprooted from his stable expatriate childhood in France when the family suddenly decamped and a life of gypsy-like wandering began – fourteen moves in ten years. His father, Joseph Burton, realised that he had to do something to provide his two boys with a stable education. This meant, if it were to be in England, the horrors of a brutal preparatory school. Used to a certain kind of sensual freedom in France, Burton and his brother were horrified to arrive back in England:

> *Everything appeared so small, so prim, so mean, the little one-familied houses contrasting in such a melancholy way with the big buildings of Tours and Paris. We revolted against the coarse and half-cooked food, and, accustomed to the excellent Bordeaux of France, we found port, sherry, and beer like strong medicine; the bread, all crumb and crust, appeared to be half-baked, and milk meant chalk and water.*

Burton had arrived in what a later writer, Lawrence Durrell would call "Pudding Island". The love-hate relationship with

England, the need constantly to escape it, whilst never quite "going native" in the country to which one has escaped, has long been a dominant theme in British travel writing. The cynic would point out that this 'alienation' has often co-existed with, back home, the ready acceptance of knighthoods and membership of gentleman's clubs, ribboned decorations and the services of a private banker or an old-fashioned shoemaker in St James. The expatriate often turns out to be the most dedicated patriot and what looks like rebellion can sometimes be nothing more than an attention-seeking pose.

But the urge to escape, to get away from home is an enduring need, particularly for the artist who is trying to create something new, and who feels constrained and hampered by the chains that bind him or her to the birthplace. Such fugitive travellers, self-exiles, cross many frontiers, see them as exhilarating challenges, tonics, excitements. There is, however, another category of those whose need to escape is more urgent, whose motive for leaving home is not so much self-fulfilment as survival. For the economic migrant, the asylum-seeker or refugee, escape is not an elixir. It is, quite literally in many cases, a matter of life and death.

★

So here I am, a couple of hours from London, travelling westwards on "The Cathedrals Express", towards Hereford, and, eventually, Mid Wales. This journey back from London to my home in Wales takes me four hours, door to door. If I lived in France the travelling time would probably be halved. Had I left St Pancras at the same time as I left Paddington I would nearly be at Aix-en-Provence by now. But this is early twenty-first century Britain where a universal network of fast trains à grande vitesse is not even a vaguely Utopian aspiration in the mind of transport planners, notwithstanding the strictly confined ambition of "HS2".

One morning, sitting in a quiet corner of an empty carriage at Hereford, waiting for the train to leave, I smiled across at the uniformed train guard. A placid Worcestershire man, he had taken the opportunity offered by a quiet start to demolish his lunch before starting his duties. Sitting at an empty table, he unwrapped a packet of silver foil to extract a substantial cheese and pickle sandwich. He lifted it up, admired its magnificent craftsmanship, then settled with quick despatch to the task of destroying it with a series of quick, savage bites. After the first few mouthfuls had been dealt with he returned it to its silver package so that it would be ready for the second bout and turned to sip his paper cup of tea. Slowly, though soon punctuated by the second wave of assaults on the doorstep, he started to talk. Waving the remnant of the sandwich from side to side for emphasis, he responded to my tart observation that the timetables had been altered yet again – to lengthen the booked duration of journeys to Paddington – with the aim simply of avoiding penalties for lateness.

"Who knows what the Powers That Be 'ad in mind," he observed with a placid sagacity.

In the silence that followed a new thought occurred to him.

"In the 1950s, when we 'ad the steam trains, the 'Erryfud train to London was quicker than it is now."

We smile. We accept. This is England.

So it is that the Cathedrals Express makes it slow, sometimes seemingly interminable, progress through the picturesque honey-coloured villages and understated, old-fashioned Englishness of the Cotswolds. The word "express" is a nice, gently ironic touch. It is like the Soviets calling a newspaper *Pravda*. And when it comes to actual cathedrals it is only really at Worcester that you get good sight of the Cathedral, though in Oxford there's a good sprinkling of Gothic towers and spires to choose from. It's a leisurely train which aspires, in a loose sort of way, to make the journey in about three hours. Generally it takes longer because many sections of the line are single track and one has to wait for late trains to clear them before slowly moving forward in that strained, heavy way in which trains take their leave of stations along this line. In the small towns of Herefordshire, car showrooms exhibit 4x4 jeeps costing £25-30,000 or more. Individual investment in private cars is immense, but halfway through the second decade of the twenty-first century the national rail network still limps along, express trains forced to share little strips of single line track with any other rattling set of carriages that happens to be dawdling along the line.

The Cathedrals Express changes its social tone and class composition in direct ratio to its distance from London. If you start from Hereford at 6.53 in the morning it's a more or less democratic travelling company but by the time you get to, say, Kingham or Charlbury the whole atmosphere changes. Especially at Charlbury. An invisible frontier is crossed. From the costly surrounding villages of Oxfordshire the well-to-do commuters: businessmen, barristers, people with loud authoritative voices, take over the train at this station, those shiny cars and jeeps once more left for the day at the station car park. Any remaining Herefordshire red-faced farmers going up to town for some rare business quietly subdue themselves.

One summer's afternoon, coming in the opposite direction, towards Hereford, I was woken from my book by a pale and shocked young man shouting:

"What on earth are you doing?"

He was standing in the aisle looking down at a young woman who had just stabbed the conductor with a long kitchen knife. The latter hurried past me, stemming the flow of blood with a handkerchief. The train was now clearly not going to leave the station in a hurry and the summer air drifted into the carriage through the open door. Moreton-in-Marsh. This is probably where you would get off to go and see Adlestrop, where Edward Thomas placed his poem about the express train drawing up in late June on a day such as this. "The steam hissed. Someone cleared his throat." Nothing else stirred and a blackbird sang in the heart of the hot English silence, and round him in a choir were "all the birds/Of Oxfordshire and Gloucestershire".

The police eventually arrived and removed the meek, biddable, mentally-disturbed young woman, who had now surrendered her bloody knife. The conductor left the train but was not seriously injured. After a long wait we moved off. Such dramas are rare on the Cotswold line.

Far more unsettling was another, bloodless, encounter on the Cathedrals Express. The carriage was not full and at the table across from me two men sat, talking in a language I could not precisely identify, but thought was Central European. Sometimes, from the train window, one sees migrant workers squatting in the Worcestershire fruit fields, the women in headscarves, making the scene look like a Balkan plain. Today the Gangmasters are licensed but back then the people who came to pick fruit and vegetables were often deceived with false promises about wages and accommodation. Many work for ten hours a day with no breaks or holiday pay, what they do earn docked to pay for crowded and insanitary accommodation, British labour laws regularly flouted. In ignorance we buy the products from big supermarkets, caught up in this seedy web of displacement, exile and misery. Minimum wage rates, statutory hours, national insurance, tax paperwork, payslips, are blown away like dry seed-husks. No one sees the drivers without legal driving licences, crop-sprayers without protective goggles, or confused and bullied workers rattling out to the fields in dirty vans.

And across from me these two hard, silent men, barely managing to talk even to each other. When the ticket-collector arrived they had no ticket. He turned to me and muttered conspiratorially under his breath:

"We're going to have a spot of bother here."

But there was none. The elder of the two men, saying nothing, and even refusing to look the ticket-collector in the eye, brought out from the inside pocket of his shiny suit jacket a thick roll of dirty notes amounting probably to well over a thousand pounds. Coldly, listlessly, he unwrapped a couple of notes and threw them on the table for the collector to pick up, looking out of the window as he did so. The change and the tickets were put on the table but still no eye contact was made. The ticket-collector was nothing, merely another disposable human creature to be used then brushed aside, of no account. I looked across at that fat dirty roll of notes and I saw what it meant. It meant hardship and suffering for someone, probably one of those women of the fields filling a wooden box with beans or strawberries. For a moment I wanted to snatch that bundle and hurl it out of the window so that it would cause no more pain but they pre-empted me by suddenly standing up and preparing to leave the train at Pershore. I watched them go along the platform.

And all around the birds of Worcestershire sang into the August afternoon.

8. Café de Paris

I know nothing about the Café de Paris except what I see from the vantage point I have chosen, a table by the window, selected to permit a view of what is going on and to make me as inconspicuous as possible. That is absurd, of course, because a Western European in Tunis in the penultimate week of a cold and wet December cannot be anything other than conspicuous. I cling to one of the most desperate self-delusions of the independent traveller: that one can simply drift through places, asking for no "tourist facilities", merely opening oneself up to whatever comes along, hoping to have cancelled, for the duration of the trip, any disabling prejudices, to have folded up any distorting lenses. Of course it's absurd. Besides, I am carrying a guidebook and between the ordinary citizen of Tunis and a man carrying a guidebook there is a gulf that nothing can bridge. Fortunately, the patrons of the Café de Paris are too polite to stare.

A few years later, in Tunis, a spark will be ignited to fire the Arab Spring of revolt, but not yet.

The waiters are elegantly dressed in blue jackets edged with a red stripe, the same contrast of colour repeated on their trousers. They are wearing black bow ties and there seem to be a great many of them. Our table is approached gracefully by the tallest, a man with small eyes set high in a long narrow skull, with a lofty but engaging charm. We order two beers, the Celtia that everyone else seems to be drinking, and he asks if we would like a dish of nuts or perhaps some *foules*. We choose the latter. He shows us how to flick off the skins with a movement of forefinger and thumb, dropping the waste in a small additional dish provided for the purpose, after which one swallows the soft cooked bean. I was brought up, however, on the idea that the rough and the smooth were intended to be taken together, so, after he has gone, I ignore his instruction.

The Café de Paris, whose name, like so much else in Tunisia, preserves, half a century after independence from the French colonial rulers, the language of the colonisers alongside the indigenous tongue, is situated in the broad Avenue Bourguiba. Habib Bourguiba was the somewhat autocratic first President of the new Republic in 1957 and at the time of my visit it seemed to stand poised, like so many Muslim countries, between the claims of Islamism and liberal modernisation. Before the revolts, Tunis still felt like a place that was living out these contradictions and tensions. There is alcohol in the Café de Paris and there are women at some of the tables but in a nearby street when I try to order wine with my meal I am told, with a stiff air of disapproval, there is none. Yet on either side of that same restaurant are bars through whose momentarily opened doors I glimpse loud voices, thick smoke, and a great number of chinking glasses. Some of the bars have stacks of beer crates forming pilasters on either side of the entrance door. *Some* people in this town know how to have a knees-up. In the city's largest department store alcohol is sold but at a grim sort of counter away from the normal display shelves. This makes everyone feel sheepish and embarrassed, engaged in a rather grubby pursuit, the vendors for their part displaying the charmless hauteur of prison warders who have come to issue some grudgingly conceded allotted ration. Elsewhere there are very French pavement cafes and, though no one boozes quite like the modern English, not everyone is sipping coffee. The bookshops have francophone and arabic literature, and there is a pleasantly civilised feel to the city. It is said that the fundamentalist pressure comes today not from the old, some of whom might still remember the French colonial days and who have grown up with the mingling of cultures and the various kinds of useful tolerance that flow from that, but from the young. Strong, simple creeds have an almost visceral appeal to young men in their twenties. The appeal of multiplicity, ideological accommodation, pragmatic pluralism, living and letting live, is never immediate. It takes longer to work its charm.

So, at the Café de Paris I pick at my *foules* and sip another beer, watching the people pass, and wonder how long it will last.

9. Floreat Etona

One of the most strongly-defended frontiers, one that never seems to show any sign of relaxing its strict and particular protocols, is the border that separates us on the grounds of class. From time to time the *douaniers* of the class system may let a few stragglers through the briefly uplifted white-and-red barrier, a gesture that merely confirms that system's residual power, making the escapees grateful and eager for the chance to be assimilated. But in spite of the occasional newspaper columnist who, in the face of the hard facts, riffs on the "classless" society, anyone who travels about England knows that class and the great social inequalities it sponsors persist. If you live in Hampstead, for example, all you need to do is to descend Haverstock Hill into Camden Town and walk along Camden High Street, mingling with the shoppers in Lidl or Argos, to see the vivid face of the other England, hardly changed since I first wandered down this street forty years ago. Although the class system has modified itself in order to survive and there have been some kinds of levelling in social behaviour and mores, the Utopian dream of a classless society is as unrealised as ever.

I went to Eton. Only for several hours, it is true, but I have been to what is probably the most famous school in the world. I am the son of a schoolmaster but I did not enjoy my schooldays. One of the happiest days of my life was the day I left school. That afternoon I was the first to the bicycle sheds, first away, pedalling furiously up the road leading to the school, out on to the main road, mad with delight. But being an Old Etonian is meant to be worth the trouble and expense. It is a serious investment. If there is such a thing as a social élite in England it must be found here at Eton and there must be some payback for the cost of those fees – around £25,000 annually per scholar.

I had been invited, as the biographer of Aldous Huxley, who was both pupil and temporary teacher here, to address the Wotton's Society Michaelmas series of philosophy talks on "*The Perennial Philosophy*: Aldous Huxley's search for transcendence." Any doubts that I might have chosen too difficult a theme were soon banished. These are serious kids.

To get to Eton you leave the train at Slough, pass through the ticket barrier, and stare bracingly at a giant box. It is a Tesco megastore, the most sizeable and unignorable building that greets the visitor to the town. Reflecting on its aggressive charmlessness I remember John Betjeman's famous doggerel about Slough in which he begs: "Come friendly bombs and fall on Slough!/It isn't fit for humans now,/There isn't grass to graze a cow. /Swarm over, Death!"

In the station parking bay I hesitate as to which car to wave at until a hoot confirms which one it is that is being driven by the Head of Divinity's wife who has been detailed to collect me. I wonder if they have a Head of Divinity in the local comprehensive. She is a cheerful woman, with that plucky, long-suffering, no-nonsense air that one somehow expects of the wife of an English public schoolmaster. As we bowl along the streets of Slough, there being nothing to detain us in the aesthetic sense, she says that they have been visited by a lot of poets but they have all been (her tone sinks into a register of light disappointment) women. Moreover they all seemed to "have agendas". The most recent was Carol Ann Duffy.

"Yes," I murmur, in an attempt to be sympathetic, "she has a lot of agendas."

Eventually we swing off the main road into a more secluded tree-lined avenue which is clearly part of the school campus but there are no checkpoints and searchlights. This discreet atmosphere of election, this confident knowledge of where the lines are drawn, would be spoiled by anything so obvious as a visible frontier post. We pull up outside a comfortable looking house which is the tied accommodation of the Head of Divinity. His father is a Cambridge professor and his brother is an editor of Penguin Classics. He is the first Head of Divinity at Eton not to be a clergyman. He is as pleasant and courteous as his wife and the terrible gaffe that I am destined to make is still safely in the future: to his visible discomfort and confusion, I will later raise the question of a speaker's fee. In this place, where only the sons of Croesus can afford to lodge, payment is plainly unheard of and to request it an awful solecism. The fact that I am a threadbare Grub Street hack with no fixed salary, surviving on modest book advances and sporadic, meagre cheques, cuts no ice. Coming to Eton, getting inside the ultimate citadel of privilege (Germaine Greer has done it, they insist on telling me, twice) should be enough. Why don't I see this? How can I be so uncouth?

But for now, all is sweetness and light and we take tea in the College house (they have a real one elsewhere for the holidays). The Head of Divinity's teenaged daughter is sitting in an armchair doing her homework. She is so clever and mature and articulate it is scary. What are the boys going to be like? Soon we are off to the College itself to find out. More and more, it begins to resemble an Oxford college rather than a school. A group of boys is waiting for me, including the two secretaries of Wotton's who are dressed in the full rig of Eton collar and tails. One of them explains that he is actually a King's Scholar which entitles him to a row of silver buttons on his jacket.

Why don't I appreciate this sort of thing more? This is England and her great traditions. Pay it some respect, you oaf!

The boys, whose manners are exquisite, for which a great deal is forgiven, begin to brief me on the rituals and procedures of their school, the liminal dangers of saying or doing the wrong thing in a place of immemorial custom and tradition. For example, it is rare, I am told, for a Prime Minister, or similar eminence to be referred to in class as an Old Etonian. It would not, one gathers, be considered a very subtle expression. Buoyed up by their friendliness and frankness I venture a question. Does a sense of the institutional past weigh on them at all?

"Oh, there's no one interesting here any more," observes the boy with the silver buttons mournfully. He sighs. "Everyone now just becomes bankers or accountants."

Warming to this theme the other boy in tails says that they were watching BBC *Newsnight* the previous evening when they heard the editor of the *Spectator* say that David Cameron, then a Tory leadership candidate, was doomed in the race because he was an Old Etonian. Cameron's talents for reinvention were clearly not, at that time, being sufficiently appreciated. The boys seemed sardonically resigned to this paradox: that the products of their institution, formerly the élite of élites, were now being judged pariahs even by the Tory Party's soulmates in the *Spectator*. I was beginning to feel sorry for these young men, especially as they seemed to display not a scrap of the languid arrogance I had expected.

We next moved off to supper and the one or two women who had been present for the fizz discreetly made themselves invisible. I looked slyly at my watch. We were in for a long evening and I still hadn't got up and delivered my paper. At supper I met the Chaplain, the first black face of the evening, who, like everyone else, was perfectly charming. I was beginning to get the hang of this very English approach to mind-boggling privilege and wealth. You treat it casually as if it were really neither here nor there and this were nothing more than the aftermath of a parish jumble sale – all weak tea and weaker puns with the vicar.

I was let into some more Etonian trade secrets like the phenomenon of "private business". Instead of the remorseless box-ticking, league-tabling rigidity presumed to exist in the state curriculum there was a system where sessions were allowed between personal tutors and a group of six boys on any subject under the sun, quite outside the curriculum. Such as?

"*A Clockwork Orange.*"

The College also owns a flat in Florence in a building formerly lived in by Robert Browning and whence Tom, the boy with silver buttons who was now acting as waiter for the evening, had just returned. They had been looked after by a master and a matron, the latter known as a "dame". Maybe I am beginning to take to all this stuff after all…

Finally, at 8.45pm, we moved off to a room in one of the older parts of the College buildings called "Headmaster's Chambers". As I walked in to the crowded room a deathly hush fell over it as if a religious service were just about to start. I read my paper for forty minutes then took questions, all of which were thoughtful and intelligent and everyone seemed to have read at least some Huxley – who as an Old Etonian himself had done some brief supply-teaching there, with Orwell and Steven Runciman as his pupils. Tom came up with an interesting theory that Huxley's adolescent sense of isolation (which I talked about and attempted to account for in my biography) could have had another source. He thought it could have been in part attributable to the special intellectual eminence and separateness of the élite group of King's Scholars who were identified by Etonian jargon as being "in College". The staff were amused at this and quickly pooh-poohed it as something that no longer applied. There's no money in being seen as an élitist these days, even if you palpably are, but I couldn't help reflecting that, whatever this tight-packed little room full of young men and gravid pates thought itself to be, it was not a group of youths in a public bus-shelter in Slough.

At the end of my talk, after questions had finished, several of the boys came up to me and asked further questions. Some bought copies of my book and one, a pink-faced youth with the portly and relaxed charm of a middle-aged City lawyer in an old-fashioned firm, said magisterially, *à propos* of Huxley's *The Perennial Philosophy*:

"I looked at a copy in my father's library."

They got me to sign a copy of my biography which I was instructed to dedicate "To College" where I was told it would be passed from hand to hand.

And then it was back to the Master's house for a glass of wine but as it was quite late and I had to get back to London I asked to be whisked to the station. It was in the car that I launched that terrible *faux pas* that made me feel like Oliver Twist asking for more. The fee...The terrible guilt pursues me still.

A group of rather threatening yobs at the far end of the empty railway carriage back to Paddington helped to acclimatise me again to another world, the one I had left earlier in the day.

10. Byzantine Workings

I have stepped off one of the Golden Horn ferries which I boarded at Usküdar and am starting to explore the side streets beyond the ruins of the old walls of Istanbul – nominally in search of a well-known Byzantine art museum, the Kariye Museum, formerly the Church of St Saviour in Chora, decorated with splendid fourteenth century mosaics and frescoes. I am, to be quite frank, lost, but this is how I like to be in cities. This way one sees what one had no special plan to see. Interesting accidents happen. The possibility of serendipitous discoveries is greatly increased and one escapes, briefly, the curse of the tourist: going where one ought to go, in accordance with the implacable rules established by the tourist industry *gauleiters*. I admire the refusal of DH Lawrence, when travelling, to "see the sights" required of him. He preferred to walk about at random with his eyes open. That is what makes him such an outstanding travel writer.

This part of the city is plainly not on the tourist route but the locals do not stare or look particularly surprised to see a solitary European wandering their back streets. It is a Sunday and, after nearly an hour's tramping, I start to become aware, just ahead, of a concentration of minibuses and coaches, disgorging people onto the street. A minaret appears, and the crowd begins to take shape. It is clearly moving towards an opening in a long high wall. I have stumbled on the Fatih Camii ("Mosque of the Conqueror"), begun in 1463, ten years after the conquest of what was then Constantinople but destroyed in the late eighteenth century by an earthquake.

This is the ultra-religious quarter of the city and, though one would hardly guess it from the brisk daytime trade in the cafes and bars of Istanbul, it is the month of Ramadan which explains the general fervour. People are pouring into the mosque and arranging their prayer-mats in the open courtyard in front of the inner entrance. A man is selling to the faithful, as they pass into the mosque, large sheets of what looks like brown wrapping paper, presumably as temporary mats. All the available spaces at the water spouts of the circular outside fountain are taken and men are sitting beneath each spout on small marble seats washing their hair and feet and upper body. A sign warns that mobile phones should be switched off but a small group of laughing, gossiping young women in their hijab takes no notice of this prohibition which in any case probably applies only to the interior of the mosque.

There is a refreshing lack of earnestness or excessive reverence and more of a party feel in the courtyard and there is much to-ing and fro-ing and noisy socialising. Later, as I walk deeper into the religious quarter, I see more severe-looking men in beards whose occasional shrewd glances (though mostly one is ignored as being of no account) seem to convey a vague sense of haughty disapproval of the infidel tourist. But in the wide outer precinct – made large enough, I read somewhere, to accommodate the tents of a caravan – there is a more relaxed feel, a mixture of dress codes for the women ranging from no special clothing at all to the generally predominant *hijab* headscarf but almost no full-length *chador*. Surprisingly, to me, Istanbul has many headscarved women (as well as those in high-fashion, midriff-flaunting Western European dress styles) whose dress contrasts with the freedom in some of the smaller towns I have been staying in along the North Aegean coast.

One of those towns was Ayvalik, where I arrived just as the schools were letting out and gaggles of schoolgirls in long white socks and pleated tartan skirts and white blouses were on the street. They might have been coming home from a traditional grammar school in Surrey. Their free-flowing hair was not restrained by any headscarf and their laughter and vitality was equally uncurbed. Ayvalik is an old Greek settlement by the sea, the crumbling houses awaiting restoration. Several mosques have artfully cloned themselves out of the residue of Greek Christian basilicas, and, in the shade of a vine outside a cafe which advertised its speciality as being grape juice from the delicious local white grapes, I met Ayhan, a retired journalist from Ankara, who owns a house in the town. His summer holiday was at an end and he was due to return to Ankara the next day but he had time for some tea and to order a plate of those grapes just harvested. He was a civilised man with a tolerant, liberal outlook and he was not completely happy about the new government that had just been elected in a much-advertised turn in an Islamist-leaning direction. He preferred the traditional Turkish separation of religion and state associated with the still dominant and iconic figure of Kemal Ataturk, whose house I had just visited on the waterfront at Izmir (Smyrna).

Ataturk, whose spirit appears in modern Turkey to be in the custodianship – confusingly for Western liberal prejudices – of the military, was resolutely opposed to anything like an Islamicisation of his country's secular institutions but times were changing.

"A man's religion is an affair between himself and his God," Ayhan declared with a weary sigh.

After we had demolished the grapes we strolled through the open air market where ancient shoe-shine men sat behind highly polished brass foot-stands that contained their polish and brushes. On the front face of these shoeshiner's boxes, in brass frames were innocent, old-fashioned glamour photographs of blonde models. Although it was a pedestrian area a car seemed to be nosing its way through the crowd. It was driven by an attractive young woman and Ayhan pointed her out:

"This is what we want, for women to drive cars. Not to be hidden away. This is the modern, twenty one century world!"

I left him, sighing with regret at the delicious-looking sweet cakes of the bicycle vendors.

"They taste beautiful but I cannot eat them. I am too fat."

The Western European complex of incomprehension, prejudice and fear – and no doubt also sometimes real understanding and even affection – in relation to Islam is hidden in Britain under the unhelpful blanket term, "Islamophobia". Such a word implies a monolithic and hostile prejudice and conveniently overlooks the trite truth that ignorance and prejudice make a two-way street.

Opportunist attacks on Western European values and lifestyle choices are no more admirable than crudely portrayed versions of Muslim culture. Nor is Islam in Britain a monolith, however much it helps the attention-seekers of both sides to pretend that it is. Traditions of tolerance, diversity, dissent, dialogue are conveniently buried under stereotypes of the single face of Islam – the headscarf, the *jihadi,* the inflammatory populist preacher in the Midlands mosque. I think sometimes of the crowds of happy and smiling men (yes, only men) I witnessed pouring out of a bright blue mosque on a sunny Friday in the Eastern Malaysian town of Kuantan sometime in the late 1980s. They were not baying for anyone's blood or cursing the West. They were simply going about their prayers in the morning sun.

If there were barriers, borders, frontier posts, separating me from those people on the forecourt of the mosque they were not visible. No one looked as though they had any appetite for such things.

A little of that indifference, that easy tolerance of the sleeping border policeman, goes a long way.

11. Writers at the Edge

In the first novel of Vladimir Nabokov, written in Russian in 1926 as *Mashenka* but translated nearly 50 years later by Michael Glenny as *Mary*, under the author's active supervision, a group of assorted *emigrés* occupy a boarding house in Berlin under the rattle of overhead trains. These include the Russian Podtyagin, whose cack-handed attempts to obtain a visa that would enable him to move to Paris (where the streets of his imagination are paved with gold) always seem to fail. He says after one setback: "Our grandchildren will never understand...that there could be so much human anxiety connected with a single rubber stamp."

Exile, as I have already suggested, is a popular choice for writers and in spite of the fact that theories of culture and language seem to demand that the writer pledge allegiance to a particular place, uprootedness seems to offer just as rich a source of sustenance as rootedness. Crossing a border can mean permanent exile but the exile is often self-imposed.

It was in Trieste that Richard Burton, the traveller whom we have already encountered, ended his days as British Consul in 1890 in his famous 'Moroccan Room' and it was where James Joyce, as countless readers of *Ulysses* have noted when finally arriving at the end of the great modernist novel (page 933 of the green 1960 Bodley Head edition above my desk) to read the signing off: "Trieste-Zürich-Paris, 1914-1921." As an adolescent in the 1970s discovering literature I read these words with extraordinary excitement. Becalmed in a Liverpool suburb, here were three exotic place-names to tantalise. This was where a writer should be, surely? But, actually, where was Trieste?

In 1999 an opinion poll revealed that 70 per cent of Italians had no idea that Trieste was part of Italy. Perhaps their confusion is understandable, for it had been the creation of the Austrian empire of the Habsburgs and it was only when that empire dissolved after the end of the First World War that it found itself tacked onto Italy rather than being bundled into the entity that would be known as Yugoslavia. Jan Morris in 2001 wrote a book about the city called *Trieste and the Meaning of Nowhere* and in 1909, when the Viennese playwright Hermann Bahr arrived in the place, he claimed to feel as though he was suspended in unreality, as if he were "nowhere at all". It is a truly liminal city and therefore instantly attractive to me.

Arriving on a train from Ljubliana in Slovenia I had something of the same sensation as Bahr. It is true that there were some pretty pavement cafes in the Italian manner. There was even a *Canal Grande*, though the canals were a laughable imitation of Venice. But the heavy architecture of the public buildings, the imperial lions and the monstrous pillars, were fiercely Teutonic and the sense of being, if not nowhere then certainly on the edge of something, was very strong. I ate on the first night in a large, gloomy restaurant served by an ancient waiter who appeared to be corseted. I watched, fascinated, as one of his colleagues arrived at a nearby table to prepare in front of the solitary diner a raw steak tartare with a great deal of rather fussy histrionics. What seemed to be missing in all this was colour and vitality. Next morning the old railway station, with disused signs still visible in German, seemed rather melancholy, as if its ornate, imperial architecture were now an embarrassment, belonging to the wrong era. Disdaining the James Joyce walk, I went to commune with the indifferent fish in the municipal aquarium, housed in a more modern concrete building on the harbour front.

I wasn't getting through to this place.

Joyce and Nora Barnacle arrived in Trieste from Zürich on 20th October 1904, with Joyce in pursuit of work as a language teacher at the Berlitz school. He sauntered down to the Piazza Grande and fell into conversation at a cafe table with three drunken English sailors. When the police decided to arrest the sailors for drunken behaviour Joyce was asked by the officer to accompany the men as interpreter. He readily agreed but on arrival at the police station the police promptly locked the author up with the drunken sailors in a cell. He demanded that the British consul come and sort things out. Ireland at that time, notwithstanding the neat maritime border around the pre-partition island, was British. Joyce's passport was thus a British one and remained so. When the consul arrived he was sceptical of this Irishman who claimed to be a language teacher, suspecting him of having been a sailor who had jumped ship, and, though he eventually secured his release, he did so with such cold arrogance that Joyce's already well-established hatred of British officialdom received another powerful reinforcement.

On his release, as his biographer, Richard Ellman puts it, "Triestines flocked to become his creditors" but he was rescued from penury by another Berlitz job, at Pula, 150 miles south of Trieste along the Istrian peninsula in Croatia. This lasted until March 1905 when Joyce returned to Trieste where he would spend most of the next decade. "And trieste, ah trieste ate my liver," he would write in *Finnegans Wake* in a phrase where *triste livre* is lurking. Joyce seems to have mellowed in Trieste (then more of a bustling Austrian port than the faded edge of Europe that it now seems) and, like Ibsen, he seems to have encountered there the spirit of the warm south. Perhaps I arrived there at the wrong time of year.

Joyce was productive in Trieste and soon finished there his poems, *Chamber Music*, the stories in *Dubliners* and the novel *Stephen Hero*, the first version of what became *A Portrait of the Artist as a Young Man*. He went on over the next eleven years to write his play *Exiles,* and to start *Ulysses*. He actually liked the easy-going rule of the Austro-Hungarian empire in the city and wrote to a friend: "They call it a ramshackle empire, I wish to God there were more such empires." But he remained an exile, faithful to the motto of his fictional hero Stephen Dedalus, who chose "silence, cunning and exile" when faced with the Ireland that he saw around him as a young man.

If we want from writers independence of mind, originality, the exercise of creative freedom then exile, for many of them, may be the only way to deliver, the only way they can get their minds free, their imaginations working in an unconfined space.

A sort of nowhere may be just the right sort of place for exile to happen.

12. Towards the Holy Mountain

The night before I left London in October 1987 a great storm swept Britain, tearing trees up by their roots and causing severe damage and flooding. Ancient elms that had hung on, maimed or actually dead, since the outbreak of Dutch Elm Disease, finally tottered and fell in many fields and hedgerows.

The next morning, as the call came from the solicitor that the deal was done, my wife and I set off in our battered old car from Bermondsey for Wales, quite unaware that, just across the river in the City, at that very moment, another storm was erupting that would lead to a massive financial crash. This would later be known as Black Monday but we were already half way down the motorway to the Welsh borders, happily ignorant of the stock market chaos.

I felt later like a scuttling survivor, a rat plopping off a sinking ship.

Six weeks after arriving in Wales and unpacking my things I was off. On Thursday 10th December, I was standing at the *guichet* of a little ticket booth on the waterfront at Hong Kong, enquiring about the cost of hydrofoil tickets along the Pearl River to China. For nearly nine months I would be on the road. Four days was the longest we stayed in any one place during those nine months. It was as if I wished to beat out of myself the years of what felt like inertia, of standing still, to exorcise some primitive demon of wanderlust.

With only a few words of Chinese, for "please" and "thank you" and "hello", I disembarked from the hydrofoil at Guangzhou, to be greeted by a small gaggle of frontier officials in cheap green uniforms and very large peaked caps. They handed me a form on which I was required to state what electronic goods I possessed, presumably so that I would not be tempted to sell them before leaving. When I emerged from the customs shed I paused for a moment. Should I turn right or left? Where on earth was I? And what did these signs mean? Even the vast railway station at Guangzhou had (in those days) no bilingual signs. I was on my own. This was an adventure and in proper adventures one never knows what is going to happen.

I decided to turn left.

I had never left Europe before and now I was crossing the border into another world with no idea what I would find in it. Hong Kong, then still British, though a teeming Chinese city, had been startling enough but China was an altogether more mysterious and challenging prospect. There were no points of reference, nothing familiar, nothing to reassure.

Perfect, I thought. That is the whole point of an adventure.

It was soon clear that I had turned in the right direction and I found myself, after a short walk, at Shamian Island where I checked in to the Shamian Hotel, one with all the trappings of a good hotel but without the price tag. I was to learn that China, in one of those brief, relatively liberalising moments, brought about in this instance by Deng Xiaoping, was enjoying a little quasi-Thatcherite turn of its own (though confined to these southern economic zones and not to be compared with the later 21st century leap forward of the Asian tiger). When I returned to Shamian five weeks later the price of that hotel room had shot up by fifty per cent. There were everywhere signs of flashy economic development, of luxury hotels, and much glass and concrete, but as I started next day to wander the streets and markets and parks of Guangzhou the ordinary people, the great seething mass of bicycles and pedestrians and long green bendy-buses, seemed to be living in a more traditional way. Some of those bicycles drew heavy loads of charcoal bricks, metal, baskets of fruit, food slops, on three-wheeled trailers. A bicycle repair man operated from a kind of raised platform on the pavement, performing his work to an admiring crowd who had gathered to watch as if it were a piece of sponsored street theatre. It was winter and the scents of meat and herbs and rubbery bicycle tyres mingled with charcoal smoke. Very poor people squatted on the pavement (though not thinking it productive to beg) or scavenged in bins for stuff to recycle or perhaps to sell as salvage; women passed carrying heavy goods on shoulder yokes; and younger women in white conical coolie hats and face masks endlessly swept the streets with long bamboo-poled brooms.

The shops sold all sorts of items from used drain pipes, tea, clothes, bicycles, to food of every variety with people endlessly guzzling bowls of tasty-looking rice and fried meat. The Chinese threw themselves into eating the way they threw themselves into work: with passionate dispatch. Young women sat on stools on the pavements with ancient rusty sewing machines or shoe-shine kits, touting for business and everywhere we were pressed to change our Foreign Exchange Certificates (FECs) for local currency. Foreigners were meant to use these certificates in the hotels and friendship stores but by changing on the black market one could get a much better rate for *renminbi*, the local currency, which was needed anyway for most small transactions in the street. I later asked someone I met why people were so keen to get hold of FECs. He explained that they enabled them to buy goods in the friendship stores.

"What kind of goods?" I asked, imagining that it would be rare luxuries not available in the ordinary shops.

"Bicycles," he replied.

When I laughed he explained that they were well-made bicycles, unlike the rubbish available to the masses.

All the time, even swimming deep in this flood of people, sights, sensations, smells, I was reminded that I was different, on the other side of a line, a sinuous, floating frontier fence beyond which was a life that I could not penetrate, only glimpse in its external particulars, sharing the wonder clearly felt in turn about me by an ancient woman with a wrinkled face like old yellow leather who stared at me wide-eyed from her collapsed heap of limbs on the pavement. What did she see? What did she think?

At one point the traffic parted and a long cavalcade of black cars with police outriders claimed its priority. Behind the smoked glass the *apparatchiks* were invisible but I felt their power. They rule in a country where absolute power brooks no challenge and political dissenters are branded criminal elements or "black hands". Money, however, poses no threat. Power can always work with money; there is a natural sympathy in their shared ends and means.

I thought of Louis-Ferdinand Céline who wrote in his *Voyage au bout de la nuit* that the laws that punish the poor are harsher than those that punish (or fail to punish) the rich because it is considered that the poor must be taught a lesson, to know their place, to kow-tow to money and power.

I saw very few non-Chinese on the crowded streets and after a long hike to the vast sprawling acreage of the central railway station I found that only one visible sign had been translated into English: "FOREIGNERS MUST PURCHASE THEIR TICKETS FROM THE CITS OFFICE." I toiled back to the CITS office only to be told that they sold direct tickets to Beijing only. I was not going that far and so back I trudged to the station. As I stood, bewildered, in front of the Chinese characters a young man approached me.

"Excuse me, please. What is that you want?"

"We are trying to buy tickets to Changsha."

"It is cheaper to buy ticket in advance but not here. You must go to old station. I go there. You come with me."

He turned back and said over his shoulder:

"My name is Yu."

He explained that he did work as an interpreter. His English seemed very good.

This was precisely the sort of situation I have learned to avoid when travelling: putting yourself in the hands of people who fortuitously present themselves in the guise of helpers and friends but who in reality have designs on you. But in this case there seemed little alternative and we followed him out of the station onto the No 7 bus. On arrival at the former central railway station Yu mused that it might be closed so he took us into the foyer of a cheap hotel while he went off to investigate. The staff immediately offered us tea and when he returned Yu asked them what a room would cost. 15 yuan, a fraction of what we had paid for the hotel on Shamian Island (with its colour television concealed when not in use behind a red velvet curtain). The hotel staff seemed to think that it was possible for us to check in but after protracted discussion they started to retreat from the idea. Yu translated. They said that perhaps the accommodation would be too simple for the foreign guests (there were no washing facilities in the rooms) and moreover the hotel would be unable to communicate with us because no one spoke English.

Yu brushed aside these objections and said that he could translate the registration from for us.

"No problem."

I started to fill the form in but the murmurings started up again and, eventually, the real truth emerged that foreigners (with the exception of the category of overseas Chinese) were not permitted in this hotel, a rule I was to encounter elsewhere. The Chinese were always courteous but equally insistent that 'foreign guests' did what foreign guests should do: stay in tourist hotels not slum it in cheap accommodation meant for the indigenous population. I was happy to go along with this. Our presence amongst these people in the cheap hotel, notwithstanding their warm smiles and their constantly replenished teapot, would, I felt sure, cause them embarrassment or expose their shyness, it would be seen as an intrusion however benign. This was their place and we had ours.

Without understanding their words I grasped the idea of the internal border, the thin, hardly visible line that must divide us, the one whose contour is, once again, so hard to trace. Yu stopped abruptly, put down the pen, and the proceedings were brought to a perfectly amicable halt. Wreathed in smiles, the staff bowed us out of the hotel.

"I have your tickets," Yu revealed when I got outside.

"They cost 48 yuan. Please, give me your book now."

He indicated that I should put the money inside the *Rough Guide to China* that I was carrying. Walking alongside me, he gently relieved me of the book. Sweeping the street carefully with his eyes, as if this were a scene in a rather hackneyed Cold War spy movie, he slipped the money out of the book into his pocket, then replaced it with the tickets. He handed me back the book, nodded politely and said goodbye. He quickly vanished into the crowd. I never saw him again.

I later learned that he had bought us the very cheapest ticket, the 'hard seat' category that is not normally sold to foreigners. China in the 1980s had no truck with sensitivities towards the Other. You were never allowed to forget that you were a 'foreign guest' operating by different rules, tolerated for your money, emphatically not one of us. Monuments and 'sights' had separate entrances for the native Chinese and for foreign guests – with separate prices for both categories. Given the enormous disparities of wealth between the Chinese and the visitor it seemed hard to object to this. And going native, with my paltry command of the language, was never an option. I would never know whether Yu had cheated us but the sum was so small (£7.20) for a long journey for two people that I hardly cared. More serious was the lack of comfort. I would learn that even the so-called 'soft seat' category was a trial and it was only the final category of 'soft sleeper' (very similar to the old-fashioned continental railway couchette compartment) that was tolerable on a long journey.

At the station next morning I encountered a fierce, plump dragon with a large peaked official hat and a megaphone down which she barked at close range aggressive instructions to the waiting passengers. We were made to sit in rows on the long wooden benches in the waiting room and told to put our baggage in front of us as if it were being presented for a kit inspection. We were then boarded, row by row, and we headed for our numbered coach and seat. I now learned that the journey to Changsha would take 15 hours. The carriage, presided over by a very friendly steward, came alive as the train prepared to leave. Out came the tea-mugs and flasks of hot water, towels were hung under the luggage racks, bags padlocked to the overhead racks. In addition to the seething crowd inside the carriage, vendors started to arrive with rice and dumplings, tea bags, peanuts, sugar cane, oranges, and other snacks. They came down the aisles, pushing roughly past the passengers who were trying to settle themselves in, and some even clambered in through the windows from the platform to sell their wares.

I now realised that 'hard seat' was exactly what it said it was. Bolt upright, backs against the hard rear of the seat, I smiled at my travelling companions who were unfazed by the sight of two foreigners. Two young brothers, both brewery workers, were going to Wuhan and they found a comfortable way of sleeping that involved using each other as props, one across the other's lap, and the other then resting on his brother's back. A fat and cheerful young man, who introduced himself as Zhang, told me he was a clothes designer. It was clear that he was being deferred to by everyone else as a man of property. He took out of his wallet a small, creased photograph of his flat. It showed him sitting on a comfortless chair in a bare room that contained only one other piece of furniture, a TV set, convincing proof of his high consumer status. Zhang wanted to know how much I was paid and how much everything cost, breaking off to take delivery through the open window from a vendor of a large piece of grilled fish which he quickly chomped his way through. He wanted to travel the world like me, he said.

"But I have only bicycle."

The passengers were champion spitters and they solved the problem of disposing of litter by tossing everything out of the window. Hot water for tea was available from a cylinder with a brass tap at the end of each carriage. We survived, reaching Changsha finally at 3.15 in the morning, which was, Zhang triumphantly informed me as he bade farewell, only one minute late. Once again I was seized with, if not panic, then a kind of wonder. What would happen now? It was dark and cold outside and we were swept out of the station like twigs in a rushing stream. Once again one reflected inwardly: *so many people!* The officious railway personnel shouted and bawled at the passengers, pushing them into lines, singling out those with large loads by pulling contemptuously at their packages and bundles. The female officials were the worst. One engaged in a slanging-match with a little peasant who carried two heavy bundles suspended from either end of a long pole. She bellowed through a megaphone held inches from his face and he screamed back angrily.

The current swept us on, out into the dark night. These are the moments in travel where, faced with the impossibility of deciding what to do next, one simply resigns oneself to one's fate, goes with the flow. It is another frontier of a kind, a brief transitional space of time between what one knows of this moment and, on the other side, the utter unpredictability of what one will find once the border is crossed. One's steps have been engaged, one is moving forward, there is no going back. I found myself out in front of the station. A noisy canvas-covered truck revved up and several passengers in this rough 'taxi' looked out at us and beckoned. We walked across and climbed in.

"Hotel," I said, a word intelligible in any language.

The vehicle, a motorcycle-engined three wheeler with wooden benches accommodating three people on either side with several more hanging off the back of the truck on the outside, roared off into the night and, fifteen minutes later, it deposited us in front of what looked like a set of factory gates. Hearing our voices, someone stirred and came to examine us from his side of the bars. I repeated the word hotel and he paused, ruminatively, then decided to slide back the gates and let us through. He led us to a porter's lodge behind the gates where another man was lying on the floor asleep, hunkered next to a small coal-burning stove. He opened his eyes slowly and yawned:

"What do you want?"

"Do you have a room?"

He looked at me as if this were a rather amusingly offbeat idea.

"A room?"

"Yes."

"Where are you from."

"The UK."

He grinned.

"Mrs Thatcher."

"Mmmm."

He smiled again at the vastly amusing thought of the Iron Lady and waved his hand slowly.

"Follow this man."

I followed his sidekick across a dark yard towards the main hotel entrance. A single light glowed softly in the foyer and, at the sound of our arrival, a pretty young receptionist, who had been sleeping behind the front desk, jumped up, smoothing down her hair and brushing off her red receptionist's jacket. Below it she was wearing only a pair of black tights, not having had time to slip her skirt back on. She quickly re-asserted her authority and the man slunk away. I filled in the register and took the key to the room. I had been shivering with cold when I arrived at the hotel but now I hit a welcome blast of warm air as the door opened and we sank into the deep, comfortable bed and fell asleep immediately.

Next morning, refreshed after our fifteen hour hard seat ordeal, I started to explore Changsha. It was a cold, grey December day and a soon to be familiar acrid smell of coal chimney smoke settled over the city. Perhaps, I speculated, this was what London was like in its era of smog. I breakfasted on a freshly grilled spicy kebab at one of the street stalls and paused, like everyone else, to admire the work of a calligrapher who was painting big black Chinese characters on a white scroll at his pavement booth. The city was vast and teeming but we seemed to be the only Westerners in town, struggling all day – pushed from one office to another – to secure a ticket to X'ian. Sent back to the travel bureau at our hotel I was initially told that the soft sleeper (we had by mutual agreement ended our affair with hard seat class) needed to be booked four days in advance. They smiled but were obdurate until I had the bright idea of pulling out one of the 20 dollar bills I had been advised to bring with me for use in precisely this kind of situation. Suddenly, all objections vanished and I was told that the tickets would be ready for me by the end of the day.

We then decided on an excursion to Shaoshan because it was the birthplace of Mao Zedong. Curiosity, rather than ideology, had persuaded me to visit but, apart from the vast mural in the station waiting room which showed the Great Helmsman founding the People's Republic in 1949, and a great white marble statue of him on the station forecourt, there seemed little overt celebration of the famous son of Shaoshan. Later I guessed that a bus waiting outside earlier to meet the train was taking the handful of ideological pilgrims to Mao's house but no one had encouraged me to board it so instead I was happy to explore a typical small rural village. No one whom I stopped had any idea where the Mao house was so I decided to order bowls of noodle soup from a friendly stall. Everyone crowded around to have a good laugh at the Big Noses struggling to use chopsticks and we played up to the joke. Afterwards I walked out to a reservoir at the edge of town and saw two men wheeling a squealing pig in a barrow to its slaughter – the sort of utterly inconsequential sight that makes up a traveller's day.

Back at the station I met a young man called Li Wei who worked in a bank, spoke perfect English, and was, like everyone else I met, an ardent Thatcherite, slightly drunk on the intoxicating idea of capitalism in the raw, which she was taken to represent. Li listened regularly to the BBC World Service which he judged less partisan and propagandist than Voice of America.

"But, tell me, what is so funny about *My Music*. Why do the studio audience laugh so much?"

I said that, like him, I didn't have a clue.

Li said that he didn't agree with the policy of charging tourists more than locals and then demanded to know whether I had a dishwasher. His dismay on learning that I didn't have one changed to shock when I said that I had only a black and white television. "Why are people so indifferent to Mao?" I asked, gesturing to the great mural that overshadowed our conversation.

He let out a sharp, scornful click through his teeth and asked tartly:

"You have heard of the Cultural Revolution?"

On the train back to Changsha a cheerful conductor led us in triumph to the privilege of a compartment entirely to ourselves – except that it had no heating and was bitterly cold. On arrival at the hotel I snatched the tickets and dashed into the restaurant, which had officially just closed, but which reluctantly agreed to serve us with a deliciously hot and spicy meal that thawed us out.

Next day the train was not due to leave until late in the afternoon so I spent the morning catching up on a few more Mao memorials in Changsha itself. I crossed the river to Orange Island and caught a bus to the tip of the island where Mao once launched himself for his famous swims.

Hundreds of hawkers plied their trade in Changsha and everywhere there were carts loaded with small coal briquettes. In one workshop I saw these being manufactured by compressing them into an iron mould. Small boys with blackened faces pushing coal barrows looked like extras in a Hollywood Dickens adaptation. The riders of three-wheeled bicycle transporters loaded with goods visibly strained to pull them and plenty of others were still waiting for hire. These included women with shoulder poles, at the end of which pans were suspended made simply of the sawn off end of a log; or an old man standing patiently behind a pair of bathroom scales on the pavement hoping for a customer anxious about his or her weight to drop him a coin. One of the street-hawkers was pushing a miracle soap that purported to remove ink stains instantly.

When it was time to board the train to X'ian I had to wait before entering my couchette compartment while some passengers who obviously hadn't booked, and were trying it on, were ejected. New sheets were produced for the foreign guests. It turned out that we were to share the compartment with three others, all of the higher official caste and thus entitled to travel by soft sleeper. One was the head of a social sciences research institute at Lanzhou in Gansu province; another was the chairman of a provincial minorities committee who said only two things, in perfectly enunciated English: "This is my sister" (the latter was the wife of the research institute head and she taught Chinese in a middle school) and "never mind". There was a boy who was introduced as "my driver" (a rather redundant role in the circumstances) and finally a garrulous graduate student at the institute who was researching Muslim history. All five, in fact, were Muslims. The lordly head of research was suffering from a heart condition and rarely left his bed. At night the two younger men left the compartment to return to the hard sleeper but, because the wife was tending her husband, she remained, making it five in a four-berth compartment. After a meal served on soiled orange tablecloths in the dining car by waiters in filthy white jackets I made up the couchette and slept solidly until, at 7.30, the radio blasted out what was probably a news bulletin followed by a high, wailing soprano singer.

I would start to get used to this voice over the next few weeks.

Unfortunately, two goods trains had collided somewhere ahead of us on the line and so we came to a halt in the middle of the countryside. It would be twelve hours before we moved off again. We had plenty of time to get to know each other. The Muslim scholar informed us that he was a great admirer of "Great Britain" and "Saatcha". Her premiership, he explained, was a marvellous example of Britain's respect for women's rights. He was of course passionately capitalist and added:

"We want your democracy."

Having quite recently resigned as assistant secretary of Bermondsey Labour Party, I felt obliged to wind him up a little by saying:

"You are a capitalist; I am a socialist."

This was translated for the benefit of the recumbent chief on his top bunk and it created great hilarity in the compartment. When I pointed out that Thatcher's Britain contained much inequality, unemployment and social conflict they all looked bored and sipped moodily at their jam jars of green tea – freshly topped up by a steward who came round regularly with a large thermos flask of hot water. All they wanted to hear was a story of unalloyed capitalist triumph and I was quite off message. They all were keen to travel but they said it was out of the question because they could not afford to visit other countries. There was no suggestion of there being any political constraint on travelling. In the course of the conversation it was clear that no one wanted even to try to defend the Chinese political system, even though they owed their soft sleeper privileges to being part of the official class.

When I eventually arrived at X'ian, where I had come to see the famous terracotta army, I found a much more attractive city than any I had seen so far. The beautiful old wooden buildings were tranquil in the cold winter sunshine, and the substantial Muslim community, whose tasty flat bread I grew very fond of during our stay, gave the city a richly mixed human flavour. For a couple of days I explored the sites and ordinary streets of X'ian. Wandering into Revolution Park, for example, I found a rather sad menagerie. This consisted of several caged birds, two tethered chickens, a rather inert thing that could have been a baby alligator in a plastic washing up bowl, two shivering and miserable guinea pigs, a stuffed two-headed dog, a stuffed seal, and another mangy creature looking like a dog with the head of a sheep. I couldn't decide whether these were genuine animal freaks that had been stuffed or merely a piece of cod-taxidermy. A rather lacklustre showman in a tatty suit emerged from his booth to perform a conversation with a row of (live) parrots on a rail, each of which, when the microphone was thrust in its face, said sharply: "Ni hao" [hello]. When this was done the showman yawned and disappeared back into his curtained booth, flicking the ghetto-blaster switch back on.

The museums and imperial tombs more than compensated for this tawdry show and on one of the great tombs of the Princess Yongtai I read with interest a sign: "These masterworks of the labouring people of the Tang dynasty also reflect the dissolute life of the feudal ruling class." Why doesn't the National Trust do more of this, silent as it always is on the life of the labouring classes who lived in the vicinity of the stately homes? On one of these tours I met two overseas Chinese, Violet and George, from New York who were struggling to come to terms with contemporary China. George had been born in Taiwan and Violet came originally from Beijing, where she had once played the violin in the Beijing Opera, but they had no recent experience of China. What did they think of the country?

"Crazy! Crazy!"

It was by now nearly a week since I had crossed the border from west to east, a border that until the nineteenth century was virtually impassible, but still I felt I was negotiating the frontier. This process hadn't stopped at the customs shed; it was permanent, re-enacted every day. I do not mean that I encountered hostility – studied indifference being the normal reaction, except when yet another fascinated crowd gathered round to watch me eat – rather I found that I was permanently being challenged by a sense that there were limits, checkpoints, barriers, that had to be crossed each day and several times a day, that I had to be ready at all times, as it were, to produce my papers. I was learning how to be an alien, someone who has crossed from the known patch to the unknown to live a precarious and uncertain existence. I was being tolerated not embraced. I was Other.

Small wonder that tourists in London and other cities and favoured destinations like to travel in great crocodiles behind a group leader whose umbrella is raised as a standard behind which to march.

That solid gregariousness is a way of protecting oneself from the exposure of being Abroad.

For the next month I would wander through China, moving slowly north but, given the enormous distances and the slow trains, and given that the Chinese winter was biting, I never made it as far north as Beijing. I was aware that I was lucky to be able to travel, to 'see the world'. In a crowded restaurant in X'ian an elderly man in a blue cotton suit came to rescue me in my confusion about how to order a bowl of noodles. He explained that he was a teacher, just about to retire. He came and sat with me and explained that he had been imprisoned for three years during the Cultural Revolution. I asked who had put him in prison.

"The citizens," he replied, in a matter of fact tone, without emotion.

"But what for?"

He burst out laughing at this.

"I don't know."

He said he wanted to travel like me.

"But I am too poor. We are all poor in China."

I went to Chengdu, arriving on Christmas Eve, and walked into the hotel restaurant where a group of senior-looking soldiers and what I assumed to be high party officials were feasting. They had their own Father Christmas who, seeing me, yanked down his white beard and explained that I had transgressed another line: this was a private banquet. I was sent up to the next floor to the Western restaurant where hideous Yuletide *musak* was playing and burgers were on the menu. I made no excuses and left and found, outside the hotel compound, a local "Friendship Restaurant" on the other side of the street where the food was excellent and where I had too many beers. As I started to re-enter the hotel compound a young man holding a carrier bag of old newspapers and magazines emerged from the shadows by the front gates. He explained that he was a medical student and that he had been reading in the *China Daily* about the Dow Jones Index and wanted to know what it was. Tipsily I embarked on an explanation involving a complex and increasingly unsuccessful analogy with the thermometer. Wide-eyed, he listened to this incoherent babble with respectful attention until I gave up the struggle. I retired to my room which, because it was three-bedded, we were required to share with another person, a young Swedish percussionist, studying music at the university, who said he was puzzled at his Chinese colleagues' ignorance of new music. His snores were themselves an essay in percussion.

After Christmas, we resumed our journey, passing through intensively cultivated fields, where swineherds and gooseherds drove their beasts and where a single man might walk dragging a water buffalo on a halter or a young woman be seen to hoe with a baby tied to her back. In a small village of mostly mud-brick huts a man sat on the veranda of a larger wooden house making straw baskets. I was going to Emei Shan, in Sichuan province, the tallest of the four sacred mountains of Buddhism, at 3000 metres. In 1987 it swarmed with indigenous pilgrims but I learn that it is now a World Heritage Site and has therefore probably become more tourist-oriented. The night before making an assault on the mountain I ate at a small restaurant at its foot. As I started to examine the menu a young man from Beijing, here on business, in a characteristic blue tunic suit, came up to the table and, introducing himself as Liu, enquired:

"Are you English? English to the core?"

Startled by this grasp of idiom, which I would later learn came from diligent study of an English phrase book, I thanked him for his offer to translate the menu but the job, after a fashion, had been done by the proprietors. When we had finished eating he returned, bowing gracefully:

"Do you mind if I join you? I know that the English are sometimes stand-offish."

We smiled and said that we did not suffer from this ailment and pulled back a chair for him. He explained that next morning an early bus could be taken to near the top of the mountain where, if we were lucky, a spectacular sunrise could be seen. Next morning at 5.30 am he came to collect us. I had been forced to argue with the hotel the previous night when I found that the water was cold. The girl at reception was bored, as Chinese hotel staff generally were when I made a complaint. This was not the done thing. One was meant to accept the natural order of things. Dissent was merely uncouth. Raising the temperature, however, I announced sternly that if it was not fixed I would refuse to pay the bill. I think I may well have struck the surface of her counter for emphasis during this pompous exhibition of consumer outrage. She yawned and picked up the phone to the absentee manager. After a short conversation with him she put down the phone and yawned again:

"It is no problem; you do not need to pay the bill."

This was not the result I wanted. I needed to wash. I needed that hot water. I was perfectly willing to pay the modest bill.

Liu smilingly greeted his two new friends.

"So you have rested and taken your baths and you are now fresh as a daisy."

"Er, not exactly."

As the bus started to groan up the mountain it got steadily colder until we reached a kind of plateau or viewing platform looking out over a lake of mist. Hawkers were touting walking sticks and simple straw snowshoes to cope with the fact that the ground was frozen hard with snow and ice. We looked out over the edge of the mountain, waiting as a pink glow appeared. When the ball of fire finally flamed on the horizon there were shouts and cheers from the crowd who then immediately broke apart to race into the restaurant for delicious bowls of hot spicy pork noodles. I showed Liu my personal chopsticks, which I carried on hygiene advice, and explained proudly that I had more or less got the hang of using them by now. He smiled and undid the breast pocket of his tunic jacket, drawing out a teaspoon which he plunged into the bowl of noodles.

We caught a bus down below the snow line and started to walk the rest of the way, through a beautiful wooded landscape of fine, dripping mist, cascading waterfalls and clear streams. Boy porters with wooden frames strapped to their backs carried heavy loads up the mountain and Liu stopped two of them to enquire about how much they were paid. Deferentially, they told the man from Beijing what they received (virtually nothing it turned out) then swung around and carried on climbing with the sureness of mountain goats up the twisting path. As I walked I talked to Liu. He lectured us severely on the transcendent virtues of Margaret Thatcher: her smart appearance, her success in making the pound strong, her domestic triumphs in the kitchen while at the same time managing to run the country, and the epic tale of her rise from rags to riches. He explained that he was a Party member (his father was a cadre) and his wife was a neurologist. He carefully listed his consumer goods: a colour TV, video recorder, washing machine, and tape recorder. He was quite disgusted by the cheapness and simplicity of my automatic camera and shook his head sadly when I produced it. His favourite video films were Westerns and he smoked very expensive-looking cigarettes which he explained were obtained "through the back door". Clearly there were many practical material advantages to being a Party member.

So here was another line to be the right side of, a frontier well worth crossing, that separated the urbane Liu from these provincial peasants.

Next day he took us to the great Buddhist shrine at Leshan where the Buddha was carved, 70 metres high, into the wall of rock. By the side of the track photographers offered to take people's pictures, a wardrobe of frilly dresses or army uniforms hanging from the branches of a tree ready to be put on for the snap. One very proud husband sat rigidly astride the photographer's horse in uniform, holding up a sword while his wife stood in respectful admiration under the tree. Outside one of the numerous temples a little knot of Tibetans, exotically dressed in comparison to the drab, uniform Han Chinese around them, with big, swashbuckling knives dangling from their belts, spotted me and came across, all curious smiles and laughter. They began to examine me closely, with wonderment, as if I were another site to see on their excursion. One elderly member of the group came up very close and reached towards my spectacles, touching the frames with the tip of his finger to reassure himself of their reality and pointing them out to his friends. There was something endearingly gentle and childlike about these smiling people

Liu watched all this with frigid disapproval.

"The Tibetans, they are very aggressive," he declared firmly.

And now we left him for his time was up and he had to go back to Beijing. We would see him again in the years that followed, in Paris, in London, even in a cheap motel outside Liverpool, because he travelled on Government business, buying scientific instruments, and providing the business support for his little platoons of purchasing scientists or local state officials. His passion for Margaret Thatcher, long after her demise, still flames, especially now that China has embraced capitalism with vigour. She mingles for him the virtues of Joan of Arc and Mother Teresa and remains a symbol of the unshackled magnificence of free markets and the culture of money. His eyes light up at the thought of her and he laughs, a gentle, tolerant ironic laugh, at our inexcusable inability to share his passionate adulation

He said he was envious of our freedom to go on travelling as he waved goodbye finally:

"You are footloose and fancy-free."

13. In Praise of Frontiers

I have been arguing so far that borders are rarely a good thing, divisive, even racist, thrusting unnecessary barriers between human beings, making their fortress cultures narrow and less rich than they might have been. But not everyone sees it this way.

The French intellectual Régis Debray, who famously fought alongside Che Guevara in Bolivia in the 1960s and has thus an impeccable revolutionary pedigree, is now in his seventies and his most recent book, *Eloge des frontières* (2010) [In Praise of Frontiers] takes up an interesting new cause: the defence of frontiers, and not just political ones.

He points out that in his native city, Paris, there are eighty quartiers, four for each of the twenty *arrondissements*, and for Debray this is a sign of the value and importance of local affiliation. We live most naturally and meaningfully, he seems to be saying, when we have established markers which indicate our sense of place, of belonging to a patch. He begins with a scornful polemic against the universal idea that frontiers everywhere must come down, dissenting from this latest in a long line of Utopian projects for creating a perfect future. Wherever possible the epithet *sans frontières*, he says, is eagerly adopted so that it can act as a form of benediction on any political or cultural project that wants to be seen to be in the vanguard of change. It can only be a matter of time, he observes drily, before we have *douaniers sans frontières* [Customs Officers Without Borders].

His little book originated in a lecture given in Tokyo where he had praised the distinctiveness of Japanese culture and its way of taking from the West what it needed but at the same time retaining its own essence. He praised, for example, the Japanese house for its system of inserting light walls and divisions to parcel up the space. For

Debray this marking of boundaries is an essential human activity. The professor of mediology (for such is the new professional title of the former revolutionary) has proved resistant to the idea that the Web is another utopia, melting all divisions in the interests of forging a world without divisions or separations where frontiers melt and are irrelevant – everything that is captured by the doubtful word *globish*. As we learn more about the ready collusion between the digital oligarchs like Google and Microsoft and the surveillance state and witness the poisonous diatribes of anonymous trolls on the internet, it can be conceded that there is much in this.

Since the foundation of the United Nations, Debray points out, far from the world coming together in a gladsome, "one world" unity, there are now four times as many nation states as there were when the UN was founded. He quotes the French geographer, Michel Foucher, who has estimated that since 1991 27,000 kilometres of new frontiers have been created, a process that shows no sign of abating. And between 2009 and 2010, for example, there were twenty-six cases of serious border conflict between states.

Debray's polemic is bracing and it highlights an aspect of frontiers and borders that I have so far not explored, having seen them up to now as problematic, as excluding, as barriers in the negative sense, that challenge incomers and create hostility towards outsiders. Debray, however, asks the question: do we really want a borderless world? Do we wish to live in our idiosyncratic *quartier* or in a world that resembles the nullified space of an international air terminal? Well, if you put it like that...Particular places, with their quiddities and little resistances, their bucking of trends, their anarchic freedom, their unique flavour, their customs, rites and local affections, are surely, he implies, where we want to live, rather than in the blandly universal landscape of an hygienic Utopia.

It's an attractive notion but it is not without its problems that are in danger of being glossed over here. It is lovely to inhabit one's own parish but what happens when some new people arrive? Are they welcome? What if they speak a different language? What if their culture, clothing, religion, or food is different? Can we accommodate them? Do they actually threaten our way of life? Is the Basque beret, worn in such a unique way that one's natal village can, I have been told, be deduced from its particular rakish angle, a celebration of attachment to the heartland or a signal, like that of a hissing reptile, that others should keep away? *You will never belong*, some seemingly innocuous rituals seem to whisper.

This was no doubt why the concept of of diversity was adopted by those seeking a fairer and more just system of race relations. As an alternative to the metaphor of the melting-pot, in which all differences were blended in order to produce a standard citizen, equal in rights and duties, pledging allegiance to a national flag, free from the stigma of being alien, diversity seemed to deal with the shortcomings of that universal or "colour-blind" melting pot model.

Instead of forcing people into a standard citizenship mould, it said, more kindly, that we could keep our differences after all, for they are what define us, what make us what we are, and no one has any business telling us how we should express our ethnicity. Even in the United States, which devised the melting-pot policy, it is obvious that in fact the huddled masses never lost their cuisine, their language and culture, and retained their distinctive racial and cultural allegiances.

But diversity itself now seems to be on the defensive. Under attack from right wing or racist politicians who see it as sanctioning too much, as undermining the essential citizenship requirements of the local or national culture, diversity is having to justify itself in a hostile climate. In Debray's own country there have been attempts to restrict religious symbols like the veil in the name of laicisation, of founding republican principles, but these moves always end by looking and feeling like an attack on the country's minorities rather than a brave assertion of enlightenment values.

The promise of diversity – that a thousand flowers might bloom – is to some people a threat. They fear that some of those luxuriant growths might be toxic because not everyone granted the freedom to be themselves wants to extend that right, in the spirit of generosity in which it was conceived, to others. Inter-communal tension or even violence prosper and just because one is a 'minority' doesn't mean that one is passionate about the rights and flavours of other minorities. Living together in true diversity, which means in mutual respect and absolute tolerance, is as difficult in a permissive multi-cultural Utopia as in an overly-disciplined nation state with a rather too well-etched sense of its dominant ethnic particularity. We all think we know what liberal tolerance is. The nostrums are easy to parrot but we are still waiting for the keys that will open the gate to Utopia.

Many of Debray's arguments, however, for preserving boundary fences are ones that any minority or majority group could sign up to. In one of his more interesting passages he points out how the perennial and seemingly indispensable idea of sanctity depends on the defining and separation of important space. The Benedictine Abbey of Ligugé, founded by St Martin of Tours in 361, has lasted so long, Debray speculates, because it owes so much "to the darkness and mystery of cloisters, little squares at the heart of its labyrinth". The defining of sacred spaces is central to so many foundation myths. Romulus, the founder of Rome, dragged his plough around the space that was to be the Capitol, in order to mark out where the walls of the citadel should be raised. He was not building a Berlin Wall or a barbed wire defence, to keep out aliens, he was marking out, defining, bringing to life, a hallowed space, created by the act of its being defined.

And there is *Genesis* itself. In the Christian account of the origins of the world (in the words of the 1611 Bible that is so lauded for its prose style by polemical atheists like Richard Dawkins or the late Christopher Hitchens) the first task of God was to deal with an earth that was "without form, and void". He called for light and, finding it was good, he "divided the light from the darkness". Not content with this he *divided* the waters from the waters, and "the waters, which were under the firmament, from the waters, which were above the firmament". This process of marking boundary divisions continued in the separation of the waters from the dry land: "And God called the dry land, Earth, and the gathering together of the waters called he, Seas: and God saw that it was good." Then there was the installation of lights in the firmament of heaven: "to divide the day from the night: and let them be for signs and for seasons, and for days and years." The stars in the firmament were to give light on earth but also "to rule over the day, and over the night, and to divide the light from the darkness: and God saw that it was good."

It is clear that, as in all creation myths, primeval chaos was being replaced by meaningful and functional order. The drawing of lines in the sand, the weaving of the Aboriginal dreaming tracks, Zeus dividing the original androgyne to create male and female, all show that the separation of elements is at the heart of the human search for meaning.

Debray accuses the "*sans-frontières*" of failing to grasp that the frontier defines life, that its enclosed space is the receptacle of significance. He calls their wish to dispense with distinctions "a kind of abdication". Were they allowed to succeed it would be a sad day for "this great multi-coloured sphere, joyously polyglot, where every day one must, spontaneously, learn to lose oneself and where one would like to be able to continue to lose oneself."

14. The Line

I am travelling yet again at the wrong time of year. In late December even Cyprus can be a little chill.

Paphos is not the worst example of tourist depredation (think of the horrors of Corfu) but its seafront, however superficially pleasant, has more or less extinguished any sense of the natural indigenous life of the place, of what it might once have been. A few old men sitting on plastic chairs out on the pavement of the promenade playing cards seem the only vestige of some older life of the *kafeneio*.

I have just caught the bus to the upper town, "Pano Paphos", to see the dusty but excellent museum of Byzantine icons, including one from the 7th century which makes it the oldest on the island. The elderly custodian has copied some icons for sale, including St Mamas, patron saint (he explains, in a complicated narrative) of the tax avoider. He is a man very conscious of the toxicity of borders, their capacity to cause discord. In 1955 he worked for the British Army in the NAAFI but, after an EOKA bomb exploded on the base, he was sacked, even though he was guiltless. The British have gone (except from the seaside hotels and the luxury villas and apartments) but the troubles of Cyprus did not end. It is an unhappily divided island where everyone has a story to tell, like the hotel receptionist who had to flee the family home at short notice in 1974, stuffing a few things into bags, to escape from what is now the Turkish zone of Cyprus. The house was immediately seized by a Turkish family. She shrugs her shoulders like everyone else. No solution seems in sight.

The icon-keeper refuses to cross the border. "I refuse to show an identity card in my own country," he says with quiet defiance, changing the subject briefly to recount the legend of the saint and his dispute with Roman tax officials. There is a lot in the story about friendly lions, the charming of snakes in the pit into which the king cast St Mamas, his coffin being washed up in Morphou bay, its heavy weight indicating that it wanted to be buried there, and so forth. These images populate the numerous versions of the saint's legend on the shadowy icons around the walls of the museum. The church built around the saint's resting place in the bay is now in the Turkish-occupied north of the island, one of only four, he claims, that have not been desecrated by the Turks. The final ignominy: they charge 4€ to enter it.

The 15th century Latin Christian church of Agia Kyriaki Chrysopolitissa in Pano Paphos, I notice, is now jointly used by Catholics and Anglicans, two creeds more easily able to rub along in the circumstances than the unnecessarily polarised faiths of Greek and Turkish Cypriot.

That night in the restaurant a string of tables are pushed together to accommodate a group of mostly Canadian soldiers (some British) in civvies. I gently suggest to the owner when he serves me that they are making a hell of a noise.

"They are on leave from Afghanistan," he explains.

It would not be prudent for him to intervene too strongly.

"Some of them are crazy."

It certainly seems so as their voices rise into a crescendo of slightly hysterical shouting and then suddenly slump into silence again. There is a sense of trauma and damage under that noisy bravado.

Next day, I am in Limassol where crowds of Filipinos are pouring away from the Catholic church on the seafront, making food or eating it from large rice-bowls in the doorways of the shops closed for Sunday. There are many Indians, too, giving the city a multicultural feel. Sharing cultural space isn't so hard. If only the politicians, Greek and Turkish, who foisted this conflict on the people of Cyprus, who were managing fine, had been able to leave them alone...

I walk into a coppersmith's shop on the waterfront and examine some fine examples of the craft: large copper bowls with heavy iron handles; *brikis*, for making Greek coffee, and those broad plates, *sinia*, that are set on wooden legs to be used as tables. The coppersmith,

Andreas, from whom I purchase a lovely little copper *briki* carrying his personal stamp on its underside, is resigned to the division of the island. He shakes his head sadly and says that, since the 1950s in Cyprus: "There has been too much change."

And finally I arrive in Nicosia where the sense of division is strongest for it is here that it is embodied in a real border. My wife was born here, in the military hospital, but the little village where her father, in the British army, and her mother were living at the time – and which survives in black and white photographs that speak of sunny days under olive trees – is now in a Turkish military zone. Will it be possible? Will it even be desirable to pay a visit? What will she see? Is it, perhaps, best left alone in the safe keeping of family memory and the pages of the photograph album?

We walk up to the military checkpoint right in the heart of the town's busy shopping street. Everything seems casual enough. People are pouring through in both directions with no obvious difficulty but when someone wanders through without showing their visa a Turkish policeman jumps up and demands to see it. The Greek Cypriot policemen are jokier, relaxed. The visa is issued to us automatically on a piece of paper to be tucked inside the passport for the day. There are no rubber stamps. Once over the line into Turkish-occupied north Nicosia, its Turkish flavour (and its relative poverty and, we soon see, even its squalor, in parts) is immediately apparent. A broad blue line has been painted on the ground (though fading now) to indicate a pedestrian trail, quite long, around the northern sector. It could be a territorial marker but it is actually there to help us find our way around, the only foreigners on this cold December morning who have chosen to do so.

We stop at the Turkish Tourism booth at the border to ask whether it is possible to visit the village. Of course, the businesslike young woman behind the counter says, brushing aside any idea that its location in a military area could constitute a problem. We are not so sure.

"This man will take you," she says, pointing to a taxi driver who is equally unfazed by driving out to a possibly restricted area.

We are still uneasy and in the end, after much deliberation, we decline their offer to go out into the countryside and set off instead on foot to explore the other side of the divided city.

We poke our heads into the Selimye Cami (mosque) which was converted from the 14th Century St Sophia Cathedral where the Lusignans were crowned as kings of Cyprus. A minaret now rises bizarrely from a French gothic cathedral. Inside, the cathedral has been stripped and painted white. It is a peculiarly ugly interior.

The Greek doorways on many of the houses now occupied by Turks still exhibit their original elegance but a glimpse through the open doors of one or two shows bleak and barn-like interiors, squalid and mean in contrast to the neo-classical beauty of the carved stone door frames.

Back in the Greek Cypriot zone we eat that night in a restaurant, which boasts that it is the only one in Nicosia run by the municipality. It is empty at first but then a large party of young people with learning disabilities and their social workers arrive for their Christmas party. A plump singer, his hair well-oiled, goes through all the standard Greek songs and everyone starts to dance. Two pretty twins try to emulate their social worker after she leaps onto a chair and starts to wriggle in belly dancer fashion (though everyone is well wrapped up against the cold). A young man does a very creditable solo dance as the dishes of the *meze* come and go behind them. The smiling amity of this little group, the barriers of understanding and communication that are crossed by the skill of the carers, warm the room.

Next day, at the Museum of the Ethnic Struggle, we examine copious photographs of "the heroes" of the 1950s and a rogue's gallery of their British interrogators who are labelled as "torturers". A British visitor has written in the Visitor's Book: "Were we really that cruel?" The detail has been unsparing. Outside, there are old British pillar-boxes, some repainted yellow and in service still, the odd one left, still painted red, fifty years after the 'torturers' departed.

In another coppersmith's shop opposite the central market the owner is ready to talk about the Turks:

"We lived like brothers but the problem with them is here. [He taps his head.] Hashish. Sleeping."

I know that I am getting one side of the story only and that similar tales will be recounted on the other side of the border.

He adds that there are thirteen copper mines in Turkish-occupied north Cyprus.

"If they worked only two or three they could be millionaires."

He has gone back to see the house from which he had been expelled at the time of the military invasion in 1974.

"They have demolished it now and built a palace. A palace!"

Shortly afterwards I turn a street corner where I am suddenly confronted with a barrier made of stacked oil-drums filled with concrete and topped with razor wire and a blue and white Greek flag. A few yards away across the rooftops the red Turkish flag with its white crescent flutters. The border runs untidily across the centre of the city, never straight, aberrant, awkward, suddenly blocking little lanes that are like the closed end of a green maze from which one backs out, trying to find the right way.

This is a border that makes no sense. The two communities lived alongside each other happily enough until politicians in both Turkey and Greece decided to make an issue of it. It is neither picturesque nor useful. There is none of the slightly carnivalesque atmosphere that sometimes springs up at borders, the riot of duty-free shops, the coming and going, the bustle, the promise of something new and different on the other side.

This 'green line' is merely dull and sullen, ashamed of its own stupidity.

15. Cross-Channel

It was, I remember, a ritual of a kind, in the years before the construction of the Channel Tunnel and the resulting swift convenience of Eurostar: the cross-channel trip. The old-fashioned corridor trains of British Rail's Southern Region, rattling out of Victoria station to Dover, the upholstery rather worn and giving off a peculiar and indefinable smell of damp mustiness, then the short sea voyage to Calais or Boulogne.

Today there are no longer ferries from Dover to Boulogne but it is still possible to sail as foot passenger to Calais, though on some sea routes out of Dover such as that to Dunkerque foot passengers are now banned, presumably for not yielding enough profit when compared with cars and other vehicles. The classic day trip of the 1970s that I recall would involve setting off early, having lunch, buying the statutory "duty-free" alcohol, and, often literally, staggering back on to the boat at the end of the day. Membership of the European Union has made duty-free a redundant goal – though some of those vast booze-barns still exist in the Pas de Calais where British white vans load up with what is still comparatively cheap drink.

One December Saturday, all those decades ago, pursued by an Australian who had been swigging throughout the voyage from a bottle of Martini bought at the on-board duty-free shop, we emerged onto the frozen streets of Boulogne with our uninvited companion behind us, slipping and tumbling in the snow, still clutching his almost-depleted bottle, and roaring with laughter at his own antics.

We eventually shook him off and went into a little neighbourhood *estaminet* where a row of impassive, unsmiling Northerners stood in a line at the bar in black berets sipping glasses of beer or wine. Boulogne and Calais are not the most romantic of

French locations – any more than Dover or Folkestone are quaintly and picturesquely English – but the point was that they were France. This was Abroad. Things looked and smelled differently and that sense of potent strangeness, that for me extensive travel across the years has made ever harder to recapture, was then still vivid. I must have been eleven or twelve years old when I first arrived in Boulogne at the start of a family holiday that involved the car being put on an *auto-couchette* sleeper to Lyon followed by a drive south to my first sight of the Mediterranean at San Raphael. The whole family changed into swimming costumes and plunged directly in. That encounter of the Northern European (and the Northern Briton) with the Med, a classic cultural encounter, has remained for me a recurring rite. When the waters of the Mediterranean close over my head for the first time on a new trip I feel that something has begun, something has been washed out and purified, as in a baptism.

As a child I gazed, fascinated, by the streets of Boulogne. Frenchmen really *did* wear black berets and ride on those funny little *motocyclettes*, with the tank of petrol across the handlebars like a basket of shopping. We went to a restaurant not far from the port before settling in to our couchette and I was puzzled by this soup that was put before me. It was clear and light and didn't strike me as real soup at all, never having encountered a French *potage* before. It should have been thick and lumpy, surely? I can remember the smell of the town but I cannot describe it or give any meaningful sense of it but smell has remained for me the most distinctive sensual impression made by a new country, a new arrival, a new frontier crossed, a border negotiated.

On another occasion, in the 1970s, I ate a large platter of *moules frites* at Calais and was sick afterwards for a week which has rather qualified my enthusiasm for that channel port.

France probably remains the first frontier that most British people cross, their first experience of abroad, though copious direct cheap flights to other European destinations must run that a close second. It is estimated that as many as half a million British people now live in France and many more have second homes there. The French statistical office says that the British permanent residents – they don't keep figures for second home owners – are clustered around four regions – the Ile de France, Midi Pyrénées, Aquitaine and Poitou Charentes.

Given these figures it is all the more puzzling that French culture has such a low profile in Britain. Books, television programmes, newspaper articles other than set-piece travel articles, do not suggest that the nation has a powerful interest in the culture of its neighbour across the Channel. Very little French writing is translated into English, French films are rarely shown on TV, there are no intelligent documentaries about contemporary French life and culture and very few people read or speak French, a trend likely to increase as language learning continues to disappear from the British educational curriculum and university departments of modern languages shut up shop.

For all the vaunted love of French cuisine and pretty Dordogne stone village architecture, one senses that the British are not really very interested in the culture of the country they have chosen to live in. The British abroad, in other words, are just that, people who bring their Englishness with them, and live in enclaves like the old colonial class. There will be countless exceptions of course but overall one doesn't get a sense that the passion for France is a passion for learning about France or for trying to penetrate to its essence.

But perhaps that aspiration, that instinct of the adventurous or exploratory traveller, to *know* another culture, is an impossible one. One can physically cross a border or frontier, shouldering one's rucksack and flourishing the travel documents in the face of the *douanier* but does one really make the spiritual, the cultural crossing? Learning the language, reading, immersing oneself in the history and art and intellectual culture of another country, can deepen one's understanding but one is always doomed to be an outsider. That doesn't, of course, mean the effort isn't worth making. We need to do better than the joker rolling around in the snow with his bottle of Martini. There is simply too much at stake for mutual understanding between nations and cultural traditions ever to be considered a disposable option. But it is hard.

Régis Debray would say, perhaps, that this failure, the sheer impossibility of successfully achieving the Utopian project of complete mutual understanding expressed in the liquidation of formal borders is not just inevitable but actually desirable. National differences, cultural exceptionalism, are not to be seen as nuisances to be eradicated but should be seen as strengths. Debray's defence of borders, of boundaries, of distinctions, of choices, of elective difference is not, as we have noted above, a proposal to start hostilities but a plea for the distinctiveness of human experience that expresses itself by preferring to exclude as well as include, to mark out space, to resist the imposition of a norm that might run on a scale from the bland to the oppressive.

In the end I think I agree with him that too many boundaries have been dissolved, that sometimes they can be a good thing, that they can make life more interesting, more varied, and actually be more conducive to mutual understanding and respect than *sans-frontièrisme*.

"Good fences make good neighbours," runs the old saw and the wisdom is in the perception that each of us needs our own space and if we are allowed to dwell in it then we might be more relaxed and at ease with ourselves and thus more benevolent towards those we share the wider spaces with.

On the British rail network there is something called the Quiet Carriage. It is a sensible idea given the armoury of noise-making equipment carried about by most travellers that greatly extends the repertoire of anti-social resources that were traditionally confined to the loud guffaw and noisy chatter. Phones that bleep and ringtones that burst out like sonic explosions (there is an iron law that says the louder the ringtone the longer the phone's owner takes to answer it); children's computer games that bleep and squeak and buzz; laptop DVDs; leaking earphones from MP3 players that can be heard from the farthest end of the carriage; and the unaccountably irritating and distracting sound of other people's phone conversations loudly imposed on everyone around them. This entire orchestra of raucous sound has in common two things: each is associated with something that has been invented to increase the pleasure and satisfaction of the individual user and each has the capacity to limit the pleasure and satisfaction of those who happen not to be that individual user. The Quiet Carriage seems, therefore, an incontestable solution to this problem. A voluntary border based on nothing more sinister than one person's preference for quietness, a border that one can cross, or not cross, at will. Moreover (though this turns out to be the problem) there are no fierce border guards to enforce the line.

I travel regularly on First Great Western whose Quiet Carriage used to provide disposable paper antimacassars on the headrest of each seat with a picture of a mobile phone with a warning red line drawn across it. Top management has plainly issued an edict to get rid of these – one can imagine the smooth arguments that will have been deployed – and the signage of the Quiet Carriage has been deliberately softened. The result is that it is more difficult to enforce the rule of silence. Those who appeal to their fellow passengers who are in breach of the rules have now to try just a little harder.

I once told a First Great Western manager at Paddington Station who had set up with self-conscious bonhomie for the day to Listen to the Public on the concourse that what was needed was a large and unambiguous sign on the door of the carriage with some blunt words beneath it saying NO MOBILE PHONES MAY BE USED IN THIS CARRIAGE. I had in mind the example of the Wigmore Hall in London where concert-goers arrive to see a very large sign mounted on an easel in front of the orchestra reminding them of their duty to switch off before the performance begins. The manager giggled nervously at this suggestion. He said that he would pass it on but I knew that his heart was not in it. In spite of the increasingly authoritarian and bullying tenor of so many public announcements on the transport networks (learned from the airports where we are treated like naughty children who need to be called to order in the raucous playground) any infringement of the unfettered rights of the mobile phone user seems, to many train companies, a step too far.

Generally speaking those in the Quiet Carriage, who are asked politely to desist from loud phone work, respond by looking around in wonderment at the discovery that they are in fact in a space governed by these simple rules. They apologise or sheepishly shrug their shoulders. A small hard core, however, are resistant or even offensive. It can be hard work persuading some people of the existence of the rules and it is usually left to fellow passengers to enforce them because the staff have too much else to do. In a culture of entitlement, the suggestion that one should accept a limit to one's behaviour is inherently problematic for some rail users. For this reason some travellers suffering from noise throw in the sponge, having resolved that it is simply too stressful to travel in the Quiet Carriage because any minute now there will be a soundburst, a confrontation, an unpleasantness. Better to move to noisy Coach B and be damned.

The Quiet Carriage, in other words, is a simple moral paradigm. It says that we cannot always do what we like because there are other people in this shared common space whom we must think of. There are limits to human freedom and these seem to involve ceding something to the needs of others. My freedom is not, it seems, always your freedom and something needs to be done about that fact. In addition the Quiet Carriage involves, to borrow from another context a phrase from the poet Philip Larkin's "The Whitsun Weddings", a "frail, travelling co-incidence", a temporary provisional government based on voluntary assent. It is unlikely that the rules of the Quiet Carriage are enforceable by law. Has anyone tried to test it? I doubt it. They depend on a fragile, but precious, civility, a tender contract enforced not by policing but by our own recognition of what we owe to others and what they owe to us. There is something beautiful about the idea of the Quiet Carriage, its founding premiss that people can regulate themselves, work out a modus vivendi that satisfies everyone. And for those for whom this blueprint from the textbooks of classic anarchism is simply too much to bear there are half dozen or more carriages on the train where they can make as much racket as they damned well like.

16. No Man's Land

I have touched on the border between life and death but it is one that we can approach only in imagination. It is more likely that a human being will encounter another kind of death-in-life, another kind of boundary on one side of which lies sanity and on the other madness – though the professional psychiatrists would deprecate such terminology.

> Great wits are sure to madness near allied,
>   And thin partitions do their bounds divide

wrote John Dryden in *Absalom and Achitophel*. Most of us, however, would prefer it if we stayed firmly on the right side of that partition.

★

The day begins with a pure blue sky that has come quickly on the heels of a light shower of rain. The sun is out, an overwhelming sense of freshness is in the new leaf and the abundant clumps of spring flowers. It is one of those days whose beauty makes us grateful for the gift of being alive. I drive to the nearby market town in a state of pleasant exaltation and, having given myself the morning off, I wander into a charity shop where, next to a row of dog-eared thrillers, I come across a book, *The Divided Self* by R D Laing. I pick it up warily, as if it might be toxic. For forty years I have avoided such books, avoided confronting, or revisiting, the state of mind out of which eventually came a determination to work my own solution, to choose another way than that of analysis, dissection. I wanted to make myself whole, to knit together the parts not to name them.

Someone else had that thought, the eponymous hero of Robert

Louis Stevenson's dark and disturbing narrative *The Strange Case of Dr Jekyll and Mr Hyde* (1886). In the final chapter of that story of dark London streets, male solitude, and quiet extremity we are given "Henry Jekyll's Full Statement of the Case", the purported justification of an experiment in self-transformation, an attempt to deal with the reality of a man's dual nature by plainly acknowledging it – passing between the two identities. Jekyll confesses that he had for a long time been "committed to a profound duplicity of life", impatient with the official face of decent and upright sobriety he was required to present to the world, and desiring unspecified "pleasures" (notably absent from this grim narrative). He rejects the charge that he was a hypocrite: "both sides of me were in dead earnest; I was no more myself when I laid aside restraint and plunged in shame, than when I laboured, in the eye of the day, at the furtherance of knowledge or the relief of sorrow and suffering". His motto became "man is not truly one, but truly two". Jekyll predicted a world to come of fractured or multiple identities a "polity of multifarious, incongruous and independent denizens". In such a world, rather than experiencing the agonizing contradictions of trying to reconcile different aspects of the self, to hold the complicated balance, the individual would simply follow each part of his or her dual self as the need arose, be two instead of an uneasy attempt always to be one. The prose in this final section of Stevenson's classic is dense and difficult. It is as if he needed to state the case that had been so vividly realised in his fictional imagination in the earlier chapters in more directly analytical or philosophical terms, to convince himself as much as others. One feels in addition that Jekyll's predicament as stated here is more closely identified with the author's own than in the main fictional narrative.

However much one might be inclined to concede the validity of Jekyll's argument, the fact remains that living two identities, being on both sides of the border at once, sets itself against another profound human need: to end the agony of the divided self, to be one, unified, reconciled person, a healthy whole. In my case the latter is a more powerful imperative.

In his youth the poet Thomas Traherne, whom we will meet again later, experienced what his biographers call a "spiritual crisis" which he described first in prose, in his work *Centuries of Meditation*:

In a lowering and sad evening, being alone in the field, when all things were dead and quiet, a certain want and horror fell upon me, beyond imagination. The unprofitableness and silence of the place dissatisfied me; its wideness terrified me; from the utmost ends of the earth fears surrounded me...I was a weak and little child, and had forgotten there was a man alive in the earth.

Then he treated of the same experience in his poem "Solitude":

How desolate!
Ah! how forlorn, how sadly did I stand
When in the field my woful State
I felt.

Traherne found a way out of this slough of despond through the practice of his Christian mysticism and became, seemingly, the happiest man alive.

I stood in the field, on an early evening of mid-September in 1970, unable to move or speak or think.

I was in Kent for the hop-picking season, my tractor stilled and all my fellow-workers, mostly Oxford students, with a bunch of young unemployed men from the East End for contrast, back in the bare, uncarpeted house which contained our dormitories. It had a dining room of rough trestle tables, and a recreation-room where a rather aloof young man from Balliol, deep in a disintegrating old armchair, would pick up his Oxford Standard Authors edition of Blake during breaks, pointedly ignoring the noisy louts around him. A cheerful, fat local woman of Kent called Dot came in to feed us, once breaking out in high-pitched screams when Tiny, one of the East End boys, pursued her with a carrot he had plucked from her basket while her back was turned and which at first she was convinced was something other than a vegetable. Another of these lads, Dennis, announced from his bunk one night that the book he was reading, Mario Puzo's

The Godfather, was "so good I want to stop reading so that I can make it last". It wasn't just the Balliol boys who liked books. One of the latter used to get the bus into Tonbridge every Saturday afternoon so that he could buy the *New Statesman* in order to study its chess problem. He also had his own jar of Frank Cooper's Oxford Marmalade which he brought with him to the breakfast table each morning.

I was away from home, the company was good, each night we spent our meagre earnings at a nearby pub called The Man of Kent, run by Colin, a barrel-shaped man who told us with proud particularity that he had been in his army days 'the batman of Malcolm Muggeridge's brother'. He had a habit of offering us drinks on tic (nothing written on any slate) and relying on us to refund him on pay day. I don't think either side was capable of remembering this fluid account. We got up early to start work at 7am, returning at 9 for breakfast and, after those boozy nights shaving was soon sacrificed. I returned home eventually with a beard that would last for another 30 years until I got bored and shaved it off around 2005.

On the train from London Bridge I fell in with a tipsy oldster who, it slowly emerged, was heading for the same Kentish hopfield as myself. Len was older than any of us, easily at retirement age, and he worked in a Stepney betting shop. I can see him, on one morning of heavy rain, half-dead in his sou'wester and cape, sprawled over the tractor's wheel, gasping for breath. Why was he here? To cure that terrible chest cough with some exercise and good Kentish air? I never really found out. I never really found out most things about Len. One Saturday afternoon, in a field behind the farm, an impromptu dog race was started. Pricking up his ears he stepped forward and offered to open a book. Within minutes greasy notes were flying back and forth. He seemed satisfied with the day's business and drinks were stood that night at The Man of Kent.

On the first day we were all lined up in front of the farm supervisors who looked dismissively at this assortment of young students and Cockney lads who now had to be assigned particular jobs. Len's shrewd eyes narrowed. He could already see which was the plum job. When the first call came for tractor drivers (whose machines would crawl along the narrow lanes of hops, tugging two trailers each containing a swaying platform that enabled the cutters to bring down the hops from the top of the pole, the bottoms having been slashed by another team walking ahead) Len stepped forward: "This is my mate Nick and we are tractor drivers." Amused by his brass cheek, the supervisor looked at him with a laugh and gestured to us to mount the two nearest machines. The Balliol men looked on sourly. Sometimes, as we crossed the field in the morning to the yard in front of the great barn, next to the oast house, which held a Heath-Robinson contraption that stripped the hops and spat out the hop bines, there would still be a fresh dew on the grass and four tractors, without drivers, their machines already started up for us, roared like proud metal horses in the soft clouds of morning mist.

I should have been happy on those far-off summer days and nights but in that 'lowering and sad evening' I felt utterly immobilised. It seemed to me that my mind at that time consisted of two spinning plates that ought to have come together symmetrically but which were wholly unsynchronised. I can still bring to mind the unpleasant and disturbing sensation if I try. There was a gap, a disjunction, a failure to connect. For many years, even when outwardly I seemed normal enough, this inner pain of dislocation persisted, it was a sense of being a partially broken instrument, one that didn't quite work, its parts resolutely refusing to fit together. Why could I not be like other people who seemed perfectly well-adjusted and normal? Why did I feel isolated on this raft of jagged emotion? Why did my mind seem a damaged, dysfunctional thing?

All adolescents experience fits of gloom, doubt, self-loathing. It is a natural part of the process of growing up. I think I can claim to have had a happy childhood, before the onset of adolescence, because it was one in which I could live wholly inside myself with my own daydreams and rich imaginative fantasies but for that reason, pretty plainly, I was riding for a fall. The transition from child to adult is always likely to be painful but I managed it very badly. I was chronically shy and withdrawn, morbidly self-conscious, hypersensitive. Even my own inner, private imaginative world that had been filled with happy invention, that was utterly self-sustaining in my childhood years, had now become a nightmarish place of fear and uncertainty. There seemed no way out of this dark wood.

I recall a day when I walked along a nearby shopping street in my north Liverpool suburb, struggling to put one foot in front of the other. The way seemed insuperable, as if I were fighting against an overwhelmingly hostile current. I did not think I could make it to the end of the street. People have nightmares of this kind in which they are frozen, immobile, unable to reach a visible goal or object. I had them in the full light of day. A disabled man with, if I recall correctly, no legs used to sit outside the supermarket on the pavement selling the *Liverpool Echo*. I passed him with the sense that the maiming I felt could not, unlike his, be seen. The whole outer world seemed alien and oppressive and there seemed no way to make a bridge to it. And always those grating, jarring, uncoordinated plates failing to engage. The mind spinning, giving no purchase. The gaps that made me say unsettling, senseless, things, embarrassing to myself and to others.

Gritting my teeth I started to read *The Divided Self*, registering its stress on the need to look at the "mad" person as a whole person, a 'being-in-the-world', not as in traditional psychiatry a casualty slumped in the psychiatric ward or lunatic asylum, waiting to have things done to him, lobotomies or leucotomies, not to be judged a thing apart, a denizen of another world, on the wrong side of the border. Laing, still a controversial figure, who wrote only a few years before my crisis, was trying to make us look at mental illness in a different way and he was unsurprisingly taken up by the 'anti-psychiatry' movement of the 1960s and after. In the world in which I grew up, the no-nonsense world of post-War northern austerity and practicality, psychobabble had no place. My oddities were put down to normal adolescent awkwardness and, even now, I cannot say that this was a serious error. I certainly saw no shrinks or counsellors, an unthinkable recourse in that world, and two factors set me on the long course of healing (I was in my 30s before I felt fully confident of myself). The first was a determination to 'get over it', to put my head down against that oncoming wave and carry on wading. Pull yourself together, lad. The second was love. If the problem of the schizoid personality as Laing describes it was a lack of comfort, both in the world and within oneself, then the surest way of reaching the opposite shore where the sand is firm beneath one's feet safely, of closing those spinning plates, was through the mutuality of human love, the daily sharing of life with another, the constant solicitation for someone other than oneself, the grateful recognition that we do not live for ourselves alone but through and with others.

I reached that shore and perhaps that is why I enter my sixth decade with such a profound sense of contentment. A gratitude for that enduring love.

17. The Toxicity of Borders

It began somewhere towards the end of my flight from Bali to Perth. The atmosphere on the plane was boisterous. A crowd of Australians in Foster's lager T-shirts ("Fosters – the Amber Nectar") who seemed rather too old to be able to carry off plausibly the role of youthful hooligan to which they aspired, ensured that the flight was lively. We had finished the in-flight meal when the cabin staff came through the aircraft spraying it against the noxious insects that we might have brought with us from Bali. Government regulations, they explained.

Emerging the next morning into the deserted streets of Perth on Anzac Day, the throbbing noise and vivid colour of the Balinese religious festival I had passed through on the way to the airport still in my consciousness, it was hard to adjust to this utterly different cityscape with its sober streets and neat pavements. I asked a silver-haired woman on a park bench, who could have entered a Dame Edna Everage lookalike contest, for some information about where to catch a bus to an advertised free open-air flute concert that seemed to be the only entertainment on offer:

"Oh, I *adore* James Galway," she exclaimed (he was not of course today's soloist).

"I expect you do too – I go all goose-pimples."

We had a Danish boy, Søren, in tow who had come with us from the airport, sharing a taxi in the middle of the night to the same cheap hostel, and when we stopped to buy something to eat before the concert at a small farmer's market he eyed the 'Danish' salami with rather too much suspicion for the stall holder's liking. In answer to the young man's question the latter explained that it was not imported from Denmark because of fear that "bugs" would come with any true Danish salami.

"This is an isolated country," he added. I thought this was rather an odd way of putting it.

Late the next afternoon, after seeing a free movie at the public library – Alan Bennet's *An Englishman Abroad*, about Guy Burgess – and catching up with English magazines like the *New Statesman* which I hadn't seen for months on this long trip, I caught a display of Aboriginal traditional dancing on the nearby museum forecourt. The dancers had lost during the flight their baggage containing their traditional dress and, since they were actually there to play a football match, the culture being an opportunistic add-on, they performed in their football shorts. One of them spread out his arms and circled the space in a dance designed to represent a wartime aeroplane flying over Darwin, their home town.

Later, while on the rail replacement bus to the out of town long distance train terminal, an Aboriginal man kept up a long, steady mumbling monologue, interrupting himself at one point to address another silver-haired white matriarch who was sitting across the aisle from him with a question too gently spoken to be truly hostile:

"How long have you lived in this country?"

"Twenty-one years," she replied sharply, clutching her handbag to herself and jutting out her chin in defiance.

The train rolled on all night and in the early morning I looked out at the red, desert landscape of the Nullarbor Plain. This was all I saw all day and when, after another night's sleep, I woke up the view was still that red, arid plain until, late morning Adelaide approached. At one point on the journey I had crossed the state border between Western Australia and South Australia and there was a rap on the door. A friendly official asked if I had any fruit with me and I produced a few apples which had to be handed over. Even inside Australia the battle against the toxic invader had to be waged with eternal vigilance. Some years after this, to help protect fruit-growing regions in South Australia, northern Victoria and southern New South Wales, growers, industry and governments from the three states joined forces to establish a Fruit Fly Exclusion Zone (FFEZ). This meant that fruit (including capsicum, chillies, tomatoes, cucumber, zucchini and squash) can not be taken into the FFEZ.

And then there were the green snails. Biosecurity, I know, is no joke and can threaten crops, so South Australia is on the defensive against green snails entering the state. This exotic plant pest was recently detected for the first time in Victoria, at Cobram in a lucerne crop and a 25 kilometre radius exclusion zone was drawn around the Cobram site infestation. Travellers entering South Australia from Victoria or New South Wales, if they are carrying vegetables with them, have always had to hand them in at the border quarantine stations, or toss them into appropriate quarantine bins.

This idea that borders and frontiers can be a barrier to the incursion of bad things – viruses, infections, diseases – is a very potent one. And of course the badness will always come from *their* side of the border not *ours*.

Later, when I reached New Zealand, my wife was carrying some cloves bought at a local market in Java when we were preparing to fly on to Los Angeles and she began to wonder if these could be imported to the United States. We went into the US Embassy in Wellington, past a rigid marine corporal on guard duty, and asked at the inquiry desk if there were any problem in importing cloves in my luggage on the next day's flight. The official looked at the sample and replied crisply:

"Cloves are good."

But people are not always good and borders have always been very keen on keeping out the bad ones, the wrong ones – though the *right* ones are always welcome. The colour of one's skin or the size of one's wallet or the ideas in one's head are relevant factors here. People with beards or Bibles (or perhaps both) were always said to be banned from entry into Albania during its years of Communist dictatorship. There's a passage in Caryl Phillips's *The European Tribe* which recounts his arrival on a business class flight at Oslo airport. Everyone passed through customs but he alone, the solitary black passenger on the flight, was pulled over, subjected to various kinds of personal questioning, of that pointless, impertinent kind that border officials love to pose, then let go with bad grace. There was absolutely no purpose to this questioning, no possible problem that a well-dressed black British author in business class could be thought to present to the Norwegian state, but the damage was done, the humiliation endured, the ground laid for a repetition in the future for someone else of colour.

In Britain it is not green snails but perceived human pests that are watched for at borders. Asylum seekers – in a country that flatters itself on its love of liberty and historical welcome to the persecuted around the globe – have a particularly hard time, especially from the brutal private security firms who have been deputed to deal with them and at whose hands some have even died. British popular media and politicians of the Right endlessly target asylum seekers and assume that the minority of bogus claimants are in fact the majority and they vie with one another to propose ever harsher sanctions. Where that visceral need comes from, to find someone to hate, some alien receptacle for fear and loathing, it would need psychiatry to account for but it is an undeniable force in contemporary societies' immigration policies. Often the same people who fulminate against asylum seekers and illegal immigrants (by which they mean immigrants of a certain type) are the same ones who announce that they would like to go and retire on a whim to Spain or Portugal or the south of France, never questioning their own right to do so.

But for there to be migrants there must be borders, otherwise we would all move in the same vast space in universal brotherhood and sisterhood, getting on with our lives. A frontier raises the stakes, cranks up the machinery of suspicion and fear, makes everyone conscious of where they stand and on which side of the line they are ranged.

One afternoon I walked into Mexico from the Texan city of El Paso, leaving behind its glass and concrete towers and rather uninteresting downtown to cross the bridge over the Rio Grande that marked its border with Mexico, to visit Juarez de la Frontera. On the far bank of the Rio Grande someone had daubed a large graffito: *Nosotros somos los illegales!* I was white, middle class, carrying a British passport stamped with a US visa, and I breezed through the border check in both directions. Immediately on entering Mexico the world changed. Gone were the sun-reflecting glass panels of the skyscrapers, the wide uncluttered streets, the shopping malls, the relative absence of people (admittedly it was the Fourth of July, a public holiday), and instead one was in a scene of wildly populous activity, where a white bus looking like something on an outing from the transport museum bounced along the street, where lively street stalls sold delicious-looking food, and the doors of a white church were thrown open to let the sound of those wailing hymns I knew so well from my Catholic childhood spill out onto the pavement.

It was a difference of culture, of sound and sight, of smell and touch and taste, but of course it was also an economic difference. The hostility towards migrants in this part of the United States, currently at unprecedented levels of intensity, is based on a reluctance to let the economic tables be turned, a desire to keep the differential, the privilege of being American, which is validated by the existence of the poor, by those without that privilege.

In Europe too the war with the migrants – which is entwined with hypocrisy because cheap, malleable migrant labour that undercuts the normal labour agreements is always most welcome to business – increases in fervour during a recession. You won't read an editorial in the *Financial Times* or *Economist* getting steamed up about cheap migrant labour, even if low-income immigration is the stock-in-trade of their customary allies in the populist media.

There is of course an alternative view of migration that says that, far from being a problem, the traffic in peoples across borders is a good thing. It enriches the collective experience, it is a prophylactic agains insularity, complacency, ignorance. It is easy to point, for example, to the positive enrichments of migration in the arts. The stimulus, cross-fertilisation, mutual energising that came about in early Modernism through the encounter of British writers and artists with Picasso, Pound, Eliot, Mondrian, Gaudier-Brzeska – the list is endless – would be a trite enough example. How many great works of literature are about journeys in search of other worlds, in search of the self through the experience of crossing borders and frontiers, leaving the natal village to seek either the metropolis or, further afield, far countries, new civilisations where new ideas could be sought, or realised. Was the journey into exile of James Joyce simply a "reaction" against Ireland or something that worked at a deeper level of necessity?

In contemporary fortress Europe there seems little appetite for such arguments. Not merely is it harder for migrants to get into Europe, they may face once they are here, not just potential racial harassment, but active pursuit by the authorities. It has been estimated that, even before the present crisis, around 100,000 people were being detained at any given time in the twenty-seven member states of the European Union suspected of unauthorised immigration and the annual numbers of deportations may be half as much again. Hounding unwelcome migrants is a costly business and the National Audit Office puts the cost of "removing" a family of asylum seekers currently at £28,000. In addition, millions of pounds annually are spent on what is called "irregular" migrants, those people who overstay their visa welcome, are refused asylum, or get themselves smuggled in the backs of lorries. These people – and as noted earlier who knows how many of them there are? – consume services like education and health. But a team of researchers from the LSE, commissioned in 2009 by the Mayor of London, suggested that if there were an amnesty programme for this group £846 million a year would be generated in tax and insurance revenues. And the economy needs them. Far from stealing our jobs they do things we won't do.

According to the international pressure group Migrants Rights International (MRI) "the most immediate challenge facing many societies worldwide now is the appalling rise in violence against migrants and increasingly restrictive government measures that undermine the fundamental basic human rights of millions of migrants and their families." In other words, for many migrants, things are getting very nasty.

MRI says that according to UN estimates, over 200 million people are now living permanently or temporarily outside their countries of origin. One out of every 35 people worldwide is currently an international migrant. This vast number includes migrant workers and their families, refugees, asylum seekers and immigrants. However, this does not take into account those of irregular or undocumented status, for which there are no reliable estimates.

"Migrants," MRI concludes, "often become universal "scapegoats," targeted for violence and excluded from legal protections in many places due to their immigration status or nationality. The increased designation of migrants as "illegal" further aggravates the deprivation of rights entitled to everyone under international human rights law. Historically, little international attention, advocacy, and public education had been devoted to upholding the human rights and dignity of migrants other than refugees, despite the elaboration of international human rights standards for migrants and declarations in international conferences calling for cooperation towards the protection of migrants' rights."

Even if the economic arguments were settled, which they are not likely to be in the short term as pressure groups and think tanks with rival political agendas endlessly contend with one another, there might also be an argument for saying that freedom of movement across the globe is akin to freedom of speech: a basic human right that frontiers interfere with. It is not an argument that is going to get very far in contemporary, austerity Europe and will have to wait its time but it is at the very least worth thinking about. What, in the end is it about someone crossing a frontier into your country that constitutes such a problem? The economic argument is the most obvious. No one seems to object to rich people deciding to live on an impulse in California or Provence or to rock stars purchasing whichever Caribbean islet or piece of Cotswold real estate they fancy but if a procession of battered caravans containing gypsies or crusties filed into Chipping Camden one can imagine the local consternation and the indignant cries in the media.

Much of the wider objection to free movement of peoples takes the form of a hostility to the different and the strange and the unaccustomed – which is another way of saying: we want this space to remain our space, taking the form it currently has. Is that also a right and a freedom? Does asserting the idiosyncratic claims of one's own patch *necessarily* mean hostility to the influx of those to whom these claims mean nothing? The liberal proposal of co-existence, of decent give and take, sounds like a solution but is it? Elective association, the gathering of like minds, speaking a common tongue, sharing certain cultural norms and values and constituting a *de facto* territory whose borders may not even be visible or consciously defined, sounds like a description of the way the world works, of how communities are formed. So haven't they a right to form these sodalities? If the answer is yes then the supplementary question is whether a border post needs to be erected to guarantee it, whether the absence of cultural *douaniers* necessarily has to result in a chaotic free-for-all in which everything disappeared into an undifferentiated soup and where no one was happy. If the answer is that it does then the frontier looks secure for the time being.

Once again, the libertarian – or Utopian – agenda of a world without borders may, in the end, be something we are not yet ready for.

18. Like a Good Confession

In his 1939 travel book *The Lawless Roads*, Graham Greene writes: "The atmosphere of the border – it is like starting over again, there is something about it like a good confession." An intriguing quotation that points to the way in which the border can become a multi-purpose metaphor and mean quite different things to different people.

Newly converted to Roman Catholicism in the 1930s, Greene (who never seems to have let his religion hamper his lifestyle) perhaps sees confession in a different way from those of us cradle-Catholics who were brought up on this practice of disappearing into a dark box to confess our sins to an invisible man on the far side of a curtained grille. I have always seen it as a way of wiping the slate clean (only to see it rapidly covered in chalky scribblings again before one has even reached home) rather than as a border between two states of – what? Sin and redemption? Purity and corruption? Black and white? Another stand-off between body and soul when, properly, these should be identical? Not so much a border as a means of getting one's papers in order in case the officials pounce on one in the street without warning.

Growing up I often felt the *absurdity* of the Catholic rite of confession, sensing that this bid for temporary forgiveness and shriving was doomed from the outset, and I struggled to take it seriously. Remorse is admirable, confession of one's failings helpful but the slate, alas, cannot be wiped clean.

I am reminded of this fragment of Greene when I come across an absorbing little book by Esther de Waal called *Living in Border Country*, where it is cited as part of a discussion of "the threshold of faith" – what the former Archbishop of Canterbury, Rowan Williams, calls: "that dangerous and transforming border between the world and God". Like me, Esther de Waal lives in the Welsh Marches, in border country, and she uses this felt particularity of place to explore the ramifications of Williams's theological concept. I am not wholly at ease with this devotional idiom, and it's one I myself can't deploy, but it is an attractive book that argues convincingly, to my mind, for the acceptance of the border as a place of negotiation of difference, of patient listening to the other's perspective, of 'conversation'. People who firmly occupy one or other side of a frontier, with their militant certainties, are unlikely to be able to take part in these delicate conversations, like those conducted in the neither-black-nor-white crepuscular light of the cloister garth. These kinds of welcome are symbolized for de Waal by the role of the porter in the Cistercian monastery who is appointed to welcome the stranger on the threshold of the monastery – a place whose cloisters and sequestered spaces might seem at first glance to represent the ultimate frontier between the secular and sacred worlds. Not so, it seems, and she quotes several voices from the monastic community who argue that there is a necessity for intrusion, for a needful encounter with the outside world, if these communities are to remain viable and useful.

In an echo of Régis Debray's argument for the role of frontiers and borders in giving shape and form to a life, of furnishing necessary and functional boundaries that mark out a way in the chaotic flux of experience, Esther de Waal reminds us of the monastic rule of *statio*, of the needful pause on the threshold, the silent and preparatory suspension of activity before entering into prayer or communal devotion. The tearing hurry of contemporary life – the peremptory vibration of a mobile phone, the unignorable bleep of an incoming email or tweet – that ceaselessly shatter the calm of tracts of silence and contemplation, are a kind of knocking away of boundaries, a way of liquidating borders, frontiers, divisions, compartments, that, if instead we left them in place, might offer a soothing stillness that could assuage that much-mentioned affliction of contemporary life, "stress".

19. Left and Right

Political allegiances, which in times of civil war divide families and communities, fracture nations, destroy lives and which have justified in the eyes of their perpetrators murderous acts, torture, censorship, suppression, genocide – an abbreviated list – can possess people like a demon. Like extreme religious fanaticism (which never minds consorting with extreme political fanaticism) political allegiance can easily become a self-righteous moral crusade, where the fact of one's difference, that one is of the blues and not of the greens, becomes far more important than the matters of substance which impelled one to to join the blues in the first place and which are said to separate one from the ideology of the greens. Angry righteousness, the visceral thrill of hating someone, can easily come to dislodge any ostensible policy agenda. The saved are keen to advertise the fact that they are the saved and to distance themselves from the unsaved at any cost.

I am in a shabby public building in south London in the early 1980s. The Small Libraries Hall in Bermondsey is the venue for the General Management Committee of Bermondsey Labour Party which, very shortly, will explode into public notoriety when it chooses a controversial Parliamentary candidate, Peter Tatchell. This has been preceded, however, by a couple of years of party infighting since the election of Margaret Thatcher in 1979 propelled a lot of new people into the Labour Party in order to resist her. Peter is the Secretary of the Party and I am his Assistant Secretary, which involves a lot of administration like typing up agendas. Sometimes he arrives outside my flat at the Borough on a Saturday night with some paperwork for me to process, his bicycle tethered to the lamp-post outside. It is Saturday night and, as someone who belongs to the Hedonistic Tendency rather than the Puritan Tendency on the Left, I am off duty. I am enjoying myself. Not exactly connecting with my Edward Hyde side, but doing what I consider normal people do at the weekends. Perhaps I am not really cut out for life as a political activist though I like writing articles for *Tribune* and *London Labour Briefing* and other ephemeral publications. The first piece of writing I ever had published outside student newspapers was a piece accepted by Dick Clements, editor of *Tribune* called, I blush at the title, "What About the Workers", indicative of my politics at the time, rooted in community action, and direct protest. The article would have been arguing for more "democratic control" (how these slogans come and go!) in the Labour Party. Like Peter I was in favour of more democratisation of the party structures of but of course in a deeply conservative organisation like the Labour Party such a change (which would have necessitated a game of musical chairs) was branded as "a takeover".

By the late 1970s Bermondsey was a moribund Labour Party constituency where in the recent past people wanting to join the local party were told that, like a snobbish suburban golf club, membership was "full up". Yet it seemed that it had been selected for an exercise in radical reform. E.P. Thompson opens his classic *The Making of the English Working Class* (1963) with a quotation of one of the basic rules of the late 18th Century radical working class organisation, the London Corresponding Society: "That the number of our Members be unlimited." This should be the basic principle of any democratic organisation but it conflicts with another principle: that those who currently exercise power should do so in perpetuity and that anyone seeking to challenge them shows a lack of due deference.

We were "modernisers" before that term was officially adopted by those planning the rightward shift in the Labour Party that was later engineered so successively by Tony Blair. Any dispassionate person walking into the Bermondsey Labour Party in 1980 and taking one look at its procedures and composition would have no choice but to say: *this has to change!*

On this night in the Small Libraries Hall the process of change had begun. Something called "custom and practice" had ordained that the votes in the annual Constituency Party elections were "counted" in a small partitioned-off room in the back corners with high windows one couldn't see through. The scrutineers would emerge with the "result", to general acclaim. On that night the unfortunate Labour Party regional organiser Kath Butler who had taken up the poisoned chalice of supervising the shenanigans in Bermondsey was there to monitor the elections. We, by which I mean "the Left" as we so proudly called ourselves, to distinguish us from those on the other side of the border, "the Right", insisted that the votes be counted in the open, on the top table, in front of Kath Butler's shrewd and beady eye.

Nothing we ever did, I think, created such outrage. There was shouting and scraping of chairs, cries of protest, but there was nothing that could be done for already we had formed a fragile majority and when the matter was put to the vote our decision was upheld. The votes came in and one by one the elected posts fell to the Left. This was naturally represented subsequently as "a takeover" and the Right tried to fight back. Frank Chapple of the electrician's union the EETPU, a notorious right wing political bruiser who had fought Communist Party influence in the Labour movement for years (there was none of that involved in Bermondsey) was exposed buying delegates to the General Management Committee to counter Left influence. The numbers, however, didn't stack up and the Left also discovered that organisations like the Socialist Educational Association could be joined and could then send entirely legitimate appropriate delegates to the GMC. One member one vote of ordinary local resident constituency party members and no others would have solved the problem and prevented all this acrimony (which even now haunts the Labour Party) but it was an idea ahead of its time.

Bored to death by this? I certainly am, but it was part of my life and although I think what happened in Bermondsey (and much more importantly in the local community battles for housing and against speculative office development that culminated in the imaginative successes of the Coin Street Community Builders on the South Bank) was at worst 'historically inevitable', at best genuinely innovative and good, it took its toll. I never liked the tribalism, the Left-Right, four legs bad, two legs good, Guelph and Ghibelline, aspect of party politics. Not all those on the Right were monsters and not all those on the Left angels, especially when, after all this initial spadework had been done, the Militant Tendency arrived belatedly on the scene and tried, not so much to take over themselves as to create sub-Trotskyist mayhem.

One day I was canvassing on my own in one of the streets on the western edge of the constituency which stretched almost to the Old Vic when I saw coming towards me a little knot of people who, it gradually became clear, were some of the prominent Old Guard: the Leader of Southwark Council (and in some people's eyes of "the Bermondsey Mafia" as we termed the Right) John O'Grady, another leading local councillor, Coral Newell, and a couple of other close allies. As I approached I thought to myself: this is going to be one of the more embarrassing moments of my life. But as we drew parallel I thought I sensed, on both sides, a kind of muted bafflement. Why was this happening? Why were people broadly on the same side, in terms of the traditional goals of the Labour party in a working class area like south London, tearing each other apart? We said nothing, made no significant gesture, merely passed each other by in awkward silence. I have never sensed more powerfully the pointlessness of so much political polemic, its divorce from the practical needs that it is meant to address.

Another time I went canvassing with Sir Reginald Goodwin, then leader of the Greater London Council and a very different in appearance and style from the MP for Bermondsey, Bob Mellish, a working class MP of a kind harder and harder to find in the contemporary Labour Party. Mellish had resigned his seat to become chair of the London Docklands Development Corporation (but also, it was suggested, because he was out of sympathy with the rising Left, which led to erroneous claims that he had somehow been unseated or deposed). His resignation precipitated the by-election which threw Peter Tatchell into the spotlight. Whatever his politics, Bob Mellish knew his people and Bermondsey was then what it would never be again, a safe Labour seat. At election times he would simply wander around the estates, shaking hands and smiling. When serious Labour activists from elsewhere were drafted in to help with the Bermondsey by-election they were shocked to discover our amateurish procedures. We seemed ignorant, for example, of arcane techniques like "the Reading Pad". This involved taking numbers outside the polling station of those who had voted and transmitting them back to a central committee room where they were entered onto long strips of paper or pads. In this way the knockers-up knew with certainty who had or had not voted that night and thus whom to revisit again and again until they had done so. There was no chance of bluffing on the part of the wretched voter; the canvassers knew better.

One night at the Bermondsey Labour Club on Lower Road SE16 in the late 1970s Mellish was addressing a small number of us ward 'organisers' in advance of the election campaign. Spotting me on the other side of the room, a new face that this wily old politician could instantly sense might not be quite what he was used to, he shot across and asked me who I was and where I was from. I explained that I was branch secretary of one of the ward parties and he nodded meaningfully. He had my number. It was inadvisable to prolong canvassing sessions, he went on to suggest to us all, because "all the old ducks and darlings" would be heading for an early night. In Bermondsey the Labour vote was simply weighed in sacks and any other party was probably wasting its time soliciting enough votes to displace Labour. The Reading Pad would have been otiose.

Sir Reg was of a different stamp, a silver-haired, refined gentleman whom I surprised one night in the Labour Club where he was sitting at a table in the empty room with no customers for his regular GLC surgery. I had come to switch off the lights and he looked up from the Times crossword which he had been solving and smiled cordially like a Trollopian prelate. On the night we went canvassing I paused at the end of one of those long deck-access public tenements that made up the bulk of the constituency's housing stock to wait for him. He would be in his seventies at that time, I would guess. When he rejoined me he shook his head sadly and observed: "Those flats are a disgrace to a public housing authority." I was impressed by his candour and sympathy for the tenants of the poorly maintained GLC block. But then I realised that I was talking to the Leader of the GLC.

Changes were taking place in the working class in Britain at that time that made much of what happened in Bermondsey seem marginal to the real event. Many working class people had long ago lost interest in Labourism and had been seduced by Thatcherism, its populist privatisation schemes for public utilities and the chance to buy their council houses. This seems today, when there is such a shortage of affordable low-rent housing, a short-sighted and stupid policy, but at the time it was judged a vote-winner. If there was truly an appetite to become property owners then the Government could have helped people to enter the market properly with free deposits or cheap loans. Instead, these nanny-state privatisations merely resulted in the long term in soaring domestic energy prices set by the privatised companies and a depletion of scarce affordable housing stock. The new breed of activists were accused by the Right, and by the slick 'modernisers' of New Labour who were just beginning to flex their muscles at that time, of being "middle class" but most were the sons and daughters of working class people who had seen their children get the education and career opportunities they had been denied. These parents voted Labour after the War with the express intention of securing those benefits for their children, so that many an Oxford-educated Left 'middle class' activist was the daughter of a factory worker or bus conductor. But, yes, there was a slight sense of incongruity when I walked from the Borough to the offices of the *London Review of Books* in Bedford Square to deliver to the editor Karl Miller my article analysing the Bermondsey debacle as it was just starting to unfold. We had a new range of weapons to use in the political game.

When I look back at that period in my life I have forgotten the ideological niceties debated on tedious Sunday mornings in a Bermondsey pub by an informal discussion group called "The Left Caucus" (who could agree about nothing). But I have a vivid memory of the people I met: Ted Bowman, chair of the North Southwark Community Development Group, a print worker from the Borough whose commitment to his community was total without being the least bit solemn or self-righteous, always the centre of lively talk at The Wheatsheaf in the Borough Market; Wally Warbey, whose cough was never improved by the boiled sweets he fed himself with constantly and who shared a council flat near the Surrey Docks with his brother where they quarrelled endlessly about which TV programme they would watch; Lil Patrick, of the Tooley Street Tenant's Association, whose immaculate council flat in Tooley Street always had a neatly folded copy of the *Morning Star* on the highly polished table in the living room; her husband Jim who responded to some duplicity on the part of Southwark Council by removing his pipe and smiling: "White man speak with forked tongue." The list could go on for another page. It was a privilege to know and to be accepted by these traditional working class politicians, community activists and trades unionists whom the Labour Party did its best to disparage in the years of Tony Blair and after. It was a privilege to be on their side of the border, the one that – in spite of talk of "union power" – divides the powerful from the powerless.

If one takes the view that political ideologies are redundant and that we are all consumers now, merely passive and obedient clients of those already cited all-powerful digital oligarchs like Google, Microsoft or Apple, before whom governments bow and scrape, then what I have just described is about as relevant to modern life as an account of the routine in a mediaeval monastery. I don't quarrel with that. Contemporary politics, where nutty populists like the leaders of UKIP "capture the public imagination" as commentators put, it is not a place for the intellectually discriminating. The game always seems to be elsewhere and, like arresting climate change, we have probably surrendered the means to stop the process, in a voluntary "loving our slavery" as Huxley wisely predicted in *Brave New World* in 1932.

But the ritual positions of Left and Right will continue to be rehearsed and slogans and taunts will be tossed across the ideological border fence.

20. North and South

I was born in Liverpool. I was born in Lancashire. I was born in a country that isn't always exactly sure what to call itself. The United Kingdom? But how united? Great Britain? But how great or in what way? England? This is what the United States often chooses to call the UK/GB, even when, like a Welsh neighbour of mine, you write a letter to the *New York Review of Books* and your address is given as "Powys, England". Giving a talk once to a group of lively, intelligent, mostly black, schoolgirls from East London they told me in discussion that when abroad they said in answer to that deceptively simple question: *where do you come from?* "I am from London." I think they meant to say that the great multi-cultural sprawl of London, a world within a world, is where they felt at home rather than that England summoned up by the poet Philip Larkin in his lines: "The shadows, the meadows, the lanes,/The guildhalls, the carved choirs."

English sounds right for the tradition of English poetry or music or language but it leaves open the question of how you embrace the other elements of the United Kingdom: the Welsh, the Scots, the Northern Irish, the Cornish, the Manx...

And the North.

My birth is registered in the County of Lancashire but I lived the first twenty-one years of my life in a Liverpool postal district. Once you start on this path you will find it forking very soon.

I grew up with a sense that "the North" was different. We spoke differently from the people "down South", our 'a's were flat and we laffed not larfed. Without being, I think 'chippy' (a word used rather too easily by the privileged) we felt – and the sociological data would bear this out – to be less favoured in the distribution of wealth and opportunity. It is a simple fact that Britain is a very unequal society and that there is a disproportionate concentration of money and power in London and the South East, not withstanding substantial pockets of poverty within that region. Politicians have made limp efforts from time to time to decentralise. The Government Health and Safety Executive's presence in my father's home town of Bootle is a consequence of this. But these days it is no longer a policy that attracts much support. The market, the faithful believe, will resolve all problems. And London is slowly choking.

In part the difference we felt was cultural and much of that sense of working by different values may by now have come to look very old-fashioned. The natural austerity of Northern families, even when they were not poor, as we were not poor, was felt as a cultural norm but its roots were often in real experiences of deprivation, a race memory of poverty. Conspicuous consumption (now lauded as a moral good, essential to continued economic growth) was frowned upon and waste was a sin. You did not leave food on your plate "when other people in the world are starving", you did not throw away things that could be mended (but modern consumer capitalism requires us precisely to do that that as a moral imperative). Built-in obsolescence, stimulation of the restless desire to dispose of gadgets and 'upgrade' them to new ones, in the process filling the landfill sites with trash, and paving the way for new short-life goods, is at odds with that old economy of living. Plenty of middle-class families in all parts of Britain, not just Northerners, practised such austerity but now it is a world that has gone. Much of the stuff unloaded from large expensive cars at the local recycling depots is merely the surplus of consumer excess not a sign that simple living is being widely adopted. Austerity has long gone except for those who have no choice but to practise it as an urgent means of survival. But these people, as ever, are well out of sight.

I have never been a stage Northerner and, in one particular, I never could be.

I call my old schoolfriend with whom I have not spoken for years, the death of a mutual schoolfriend prompting the call.

"I didn't know it was you," he says.

I know it is him. I hear, incidentally, the unmistakeable Liverpool accent in which a thousand witty phrases were delivered when we were best mates at school, I recall his gift for brilliant linguistic play that dazzled the Oxford entrance examiners and won him an Exhibitioner's gown.

"You sounded like a Southerner."

After all these years, does it matter? Who cares what I sound like? The answer is that many still do. Holding fast to a regional accent, especially a Northern one, is a mark of integrity, of loyalty to place, of refusal to compromise with the ruddy Southerners. I know this, and half believe it still. I never consciously tried to fix my accent, like the famous Northern TV presenter who disappeared into her room in her first term at Cambridge, to emerge a few weeks later with a wholly reconstructed 'Southern' accent. I am not ashamed of the traces of Northern speech which a moderately attentive listener could quickly detect anyway, especially those flat 'a's I obstinately cling to. I never tried to alter the way I spoke but thirty years away, thirty years of living out of the North, thirty years of work initially as an information officer, answering an official phone, thirty years of public speaking, lecturing, holding forth at literary festivals, reading my poems, teaching, have abraded the traces (never anywhere near as strong as my friend's) of my original Scouse intonation. Why does one have a particular accent in the first place? Because that is how everyone around one is speaking. Change the ambience and the way of speaking changes. This is part of the explanation (though some regional accents are more tenacious than others) but it isn't the whole story.

I haven't yet got to the bottom of this.

I could appeal to the professional socio-linguists but I don't think the answer lies that way.

I am in a recording studio, reading the entire text of my book of poems, *Acapulco* for the audio company *Spoken Ink*. It will take two hours, every fluff and uncertainty, every unclear syllable, being relentlessly re-recorded to get it absolutely right. But the producer, Constantine, says after only a few minutes:

"The microphone likes your voice."

If that is true then isn't it worth getting it right? But why should getting it right mean changing the regional flavour? It would be unthinkable to listen to an audio recording of Seamus Heaney or Douglas Dunn without, respectively, their Irish and Scottish verbal music being central to the experience of hearing.

In the past one would change one's accent, learn to speak proper, or 'posh', in order to advance oneself. Could this really be what I have done? Or is my 'abrading' thesis more likely to be the answer, a withering away from lack of use?

The really interesting question, perhaps, is why I bother my head with the issue. Would anyone in the United States, for example, waste time on this? Sure, a New York editor doesn't sound like a redneck farmer driving a pickup truck in Alabama but would very many in the States outside the old East Coast elites consider the way one spoke an issue of real importance?

In the end, I decide it has nothing to do with utility or opportunity. It is, at some level I can hardly reach in order to articulate it, a matter of visceral loyalty to what I was and what I have lost, for there is always loss, and the traces of what has gone linger like the effect of a vibrating string in the silence when the music stops.

21. Lost in Translation

" Poetry," said Robert Frost, in an aphorism that has probably been quoted too often for its own good, "is what gets lost in translation." His meaning is clear enough: in a poem language is under maximum creative pressure and the words, even the syllables, chosen are so vital and unique to the moment of its making that only these words will do and no others. Translation cannot hope to capture the uniqueness of that linguistic act and must always be an approximation.

It is easy enough to refute Frost in the sense that if we took what he said literally much of world literature would be inaccessible to us. There would be in place an iron linguistic curtain that concealed something vital. Poetry in a parallel text or with a prose gloss at the foot of the page like the wonderful old *Penguin Book of French Verse*, is fine for Europeans with a smattering of French, Spanish, Italian, German but what of Chinese, Russian, Arabic, African languages? Without translation we would be missing out on great works of the imagination. And why grant a special privilege to poetry? Surely the best and most creative fiction shares that unique linguistic authenticity? The French novelist Jean-Philippe Toussaint, in his recent book *L'urgence et la patience* has an electrifying account of the writing process, as intense as any description I have ever read of the act of poetic creation.

All truly creative writing is unique to the moment of its making.

Such arguments also belittle the art of translation which can actually add to – some would argue on occasion improve – the original. Translation is not a matter of transferring some paraphrasable content from one language to another like a parcel passed from hand to hand. It is, as every good translator knows, a recreation, a new departure which is at the same time 'faithful' in the proper sense. Translation, as Matthew Arnold wrote, aims at "reproducing the effect" of the original so that we know it, as near as we possibly can, as the reader in the original language knew it.

I have kept returning for years to a slim, now dog-eared, Penguin Classic volume of three Abbasid poets translated by Abdullah Al-Udhari and George Wightman as *Birds Through a Ceiling of Alabaster*. Without translators such poetry would be closed to me and those poetic voices forever unheard. And then there are the other encounters of poets with other poets that are not translations proper, rather creative engagements, like Peter Reading's inspired reactions to the Latin poet Propertius, or Alice Oswald's reworking of the themes of the *Iliad*. Poetry is a dialogue, an engagement, with readers and the world and the tradition which is universal, not in the sense of dwelling in that bland and featureless Globish we have already encountered, but in sharing an inheritance of ideas, images, myths: the ground and being of poetry.

And yet…Somehow this won't do. Language itself seems to resist such confident universalizing. Esperanto remains a hopeful aspiration. Left to itself, a language will weave all sorts of intricate patterns, create idioms, slang, jargons, opaque particularities, that delight its native speakers but which make things difficult – and is this not rather the point? – for those who do not speak that language. Language, we confidently say, is concerned primarily with communication. But is it? Does it not love instead the sly, the devious, the suggestive, the glancing? Does it not like to nod to the initiate? Are not the pleasures of concealment, code, the covert, just as attractive as candour and lucidity? Is not making oneself plain a lot less fun than making oneself playfully enigmatic? Each language has a genius, an inner motion, a deep source that even the tolerably competent multilingualist may be able to approach only in an approximate way.

Even dialectical pronunciations, or regional accents that pose no barriers (usually!) to understanding are part of this process of individuation. If we all sounded like 1950s BBC announcers spoken English would be a lot less fun. Once again, the tendency of human activities like language to go their own particular way fatally undermines the Utopian project.

In his latest book, George Steiner, author of *After Babel*, writes: "To learn a language is to expand incommensurably the parochialism of the self. It is to fling open a new window on existence." It is to crash through that red-and-white metal barrier erected by the linguistic frontier officials.

I want to see fewer borders, more eager coming and going, more sharing of experience, language, culture, being. I shall never learn to love frontier crossings, visas, immigration rules, the rubber stamp, the hostile scrutiny, the churlishly reluctant nod of the head that allows one through the barrier – and all the pain and suffering of the migrant across the globe and down the ages.

But not yet the borderless world, the realisation on earth of globalization's dream, of life *sans frontières*. In the face of the world's Googleisation, the Net's imperious imposition of uniformity and our eager embrace of it, let us cling a little longer to difference, quiddity, the eccentric and the recalcitrant. Let us exercise that most precious of freedoms, the core freedom on which all others depend: the untrammelled, unauthorised, capacity to say *no*.

To draw a line in the white sand.

Part Two:
Living in Border Country

1. Renewal

They have arrived.

A scuffling and chattering and squeaking outside the bedroom window confirms that the house martins have completed their migration from sub-Saharan Africa, flying by day with their mouths open to feed on airborne insects, performing their annual migratory marvel. Sweeping in across the valley they come to rest beneath the eaves of my cottage. They may find there the vestige of last year's nests, built up from gobs of chewed mud that they have spat out from their beaks to form a bulbous hive, its texture that of a thickly-knitted woollen beanie. They move quickly and busily, hoping to defeat the sparrows who are known to hijack half built nests for their own purposes. If the martins can close the entrance of the nest in time it will prove resistant to that invader.

Eight or nine of these nests – some now untenanted as numbers fall – cling beneath the eaves that face south-east into the valley, the base plinth of the front wall smeared all summer long with thick streaks and splashes of bird-lime.

So we are woken at dawn by fidgeting and scratching. The martins are at their nest-building, and the opportunistic sparrows are picking at the putty that secures the glass of the window-pane in search of an insect, a bright eye sometimes peering curiously in at us. The martins' swooping flight is sometimes completed in one single arc that ends in touch-down at the nest, sometimes arrested in an abrupt last-minute withdrawal – especially if they sense that they are being watched.

Banquo, in *Macbeth*, drew these birds to the attention of Duncan at Macbeth's castle:

This guest of summer,
The temple-haunting martlet, does approve
By his loved mansionry that the heaven's breath
Smells wooingly here. No jutty, frieze,
Buttress, nor coign of vantage, but this bird
Hath made his pendant bed and procreant cradle;
Where they most breed and haunt, I have observed
The air is delicate.

The air is delicate. It is April, but Spring comes later on the higher ground of the Welsh Marches. The apple-blossom is already out in the orchards of Herefordshire only a dozen or so miles away but in Radnorshire our tight buds are only now beginning to unclench on the ragged Bramleys. An Ordnance Survey spot height on the map confirms that the martins have chosen their summer *hafod* at 300 metres above sea level, just short of 1000 feet.

A ragged hawthorn bush on the far side of the lane is visible from my bedroom window. For twenty-five years I have watched, each breaking season, the bare winter branches suddenly sprout green leaf. Hedges in the contemporary countryside are rarely allowed to be this untidy. In the late autumn the tractors come with their long slashing flails to shave the hedgerows into neat lines, the sound of their crackling and spitting out of splintered debris filling the still, smoke-scented air of a late November afternoon. I have never asked why this stretch of hedge in front of the cottage, that turns at a sharp right-angle and runs down alongside the steep lane that falls to the village, has been allowed to grow wild but there it is, performing for me its annual rite of confirmation.

2. Tracing the Frontier

Somewhere between four and five o'clock in the morning I have started, very slowly, to become aware of another border. But I do not yet know where I am.

I am suspended at the shadowy frontier between sleep and waking consciousness. I am being carried forward like a swimmer brought to the shore by a powerful wave. Very soon my feet will feel the smooth stones of a steep and shelving shingle beach, but for now I am still at the threshold, in a drifting nowhere.

If the imagery of dreams is fantastic and lurid, they are always rooted in a very powerful sense of reality. Dream reality is exaggerated, parodied, hammed-up, made garish, but nevertheless exists behind the soaring flights, the fearful horrors, the naked exposure, the dread. It is ultimately responsible for this freak show. It is calling the shots. Perhaps this is why we often live our dreams with a greater urgency than the daily life they dissolve into.

This morning the aftermath of my dream – the projection of some long-hugged anxiety – is still with me. The metaphor of swimming seems appropriate. One is in an enveloping element and one is in motion.

Then there is a sound that seems to speak of something more present and urgent. It is not from the world of dreams. It is real. I am waking at last but I still have not yet reached a definite conclusion about where I am. Somewhere, I am now convinced, a blackbird is calling and I lie still, letting my mind gather itself in order to pronounce the definitive verdict. Then, finally, my eyes open. It is dark in the room. I look from one side to the other. The source of the new day's light is what will, ultimately, confirm for me where I am.

What I am hearing is a single chirping, not the richly populated orchestra of a full dawn chorus, and it struggles to compete with the heavy, grinding rumble and brake-hiss of a large delivery truck that passes the bird's refuge at the heart of a London plane tree.

The question is resolved. I am in the centre of London in my tiny studio flat, a stone's throw from Russell Square, on a busy north-south artery taking traffic all night long (with only the briefest of pauses for an hour at most between four and five a.m.) from north London towards the Thames, in-car sound thumping out at disco levels, revellers shouting, crack-heads bellowing obscenities, brakes snorting and spitting, police and ambulance sirens screaming at extraordinary volume and with hysterical stridency.

And the lone blackbird, confused by artificial light, struggling to make itself heard above the din.

Plainly, I am not at my Welsh home, where the authentic orchestration of the dawn chorus would have emerged, softly, from a still, nocturnal silence that would have been interrupted if at all only by the soft hooting of an owl in the tall ash. But I have lain there too, in a similar state of liminal doubt, waiting for confirmation of where I am.

The human need to know who we are and where we belong, is as urgent and implacable as all our other needs. Finding the answer, finding the place where we are from, involves the negotiation of borders, of definitions, distinctions, demarcations. It demands the drawing of lines in the sand, the erection of fences, the establishment of crossing-places.

Wherever we live we put down deep tap-roots – a holiday villa becomes after a few days as familiar as an old shoe – as if it were intended that we should always choose a habitat and stick to it. Even the nomad's tent – Bruce Chatwin's symbol of the human need to wander in order to drink from the proper source of life – is fiercely individuated, with its silver coffee pots and precious rugs laid out on the sandy floor.

I should not be surprised that this strange life I lead, shuttling between two beds, frequently confuses and disorients me. My regular crossings are not just between two countries, England and Wales, they are between two different modes of being, maybe even two different personalities.

It does not end there.

It is not just that I carry a physical body through the ticket barrier at Paddington or that I bring my ordinary material self along the railways and roads that I traverse, to culminate yet again in the sight of that roadside sign *Croeso y Cymru*.

I can cross the border without leaving home. I can feel, and have always felt, that a frontier fence runs through my own self

This fence is crooked, concealed in parts under rampant thistle and long grass, in other places exposed, hard to follow with confident precision and generally neglected by the telescopic sights of those intermittently watchful, though generally indifferent, border guards. But it has always felt very real and I don't imagine for a second that it makes me unique or even unusual. Those who possess a confident sense of belonging, who know who they are and where they are and what are the boundaries of their territory, untroubled by divided loyalties or inner conflicts of allegiance and attachment, who experience no anxiety at the looming presence of a border post, literal or metaphorical, are the lucky ones. They may also be in a minority.

I have written this book to find out why I am not of their number.

3. Along the Border

I am on the beach at Prestatyn in North Wales at the start (or the finish) of the Offa's Dyke long distance footpath (Llwybr Clawdd Offa). From the various walker's guides it is clear that the preferred direction of travel is from the south at Chepstow northwards, finishing on this flat beach facing the Liverpool Bay with, to the west, a distant view of the mountains of Snowdonia. If you are lucky and the great peak of Snowdon is not hiding behind cloud or mist you will see it, Yr Wyddfa, towering over its neighbours.

It's a bright day so we push off valiantly. Determined walkers can complete the 182 mile path to Cas Gwent in a couple of weeks but I am not a determined walker. Getting from A to B is much less interesting to me than what happens along the way and all the digressions and diversions and non-sequiturs (the posh word for getting lost) that one has to look forward to. Today I am just tackling a short stretch of the path, having walked in the past from the start at Chepstow as far as Welshpool – *nel mezzo del cammin* – in stages, at different times. Some other day I will close the gap between where I fetch up today and Welshpool. It's something to look forward to.

I haven't been going long before someone in proper tackle and a very impressive pair of boots shoots past with a cheerful greeting that enfolds also some sly, mute disapproval of my lax attitude. Or am I imagining that? Of course I am. At the same time it is true that no one now walks as Wordsworth or the Victorians did, in ordinary get-up. George Borrow, who walked hundreds of miles of 'Wild Wales' in the 19th Century, actually *carried an umbrella*. Walking, like all other country pursuits, as Aldous Huxley presciently imagined in *Brave New World* in 1932, is a serious business with serious equipment designed to make a lot of people a lot of money. You don't just put on a pair of stout shoes and start placing one foot in front of the other. You must be properly kitted out and do the thing properly. The protocols of late capitalist consumerism demand this; resistance is out of the question.

The dyke built by Offa, the 8th century King of Mercia, to keep the Welsh out of his kingdom, still survives, impressively, in places. It's thrilling to walk along an earthwork of such ancient lineage and one can often do so, but not along this northern stretch which has been designed, reasonably enough, to give good walking rather than to follow slavishly the route of the original dyke. And no doubt hard factors like land ownership, rights of way, and access play their part. The consolation is that the walk passes through the beautiful Vale of Clwyd. On the map I see that the border between the counties of Denbighshire and Cheshire is a wavy line drawn in the middle of the Dee estuary so it's just as well that I wasn't planning to walk literally along the border. That would have involved a visit to the 'adventure clothing' boutique for a wet suit.

The designated trail leads up from Prestatyn beach into town. It's always hard to resist the lure of charity shops but it's early enough for them not to be open yet. The high street, it turns out, isn't just the usual desolate array of charity shops, junk food outlets, pound shops, and boarded-up shopfronts scribbled all over with graffiti. There seem to be plenty of interesting small businesses and a refreshing absence of the dominant chain stores. Those seem to have been mostly coralled in a large Retail Park a few streets away.

Eventually, after the high street falls away, Offa's trail leads into pure suburbia and then the gradient quickly increases. Those promised views turn out to entail getting yourself up to the viewpoint in short order, puffing and gasping after a 33% climb that even the motorists seem to be struggling with, but the view from the first vantage point is excellent: the beach and the hills and the distant mountains are all laid out like a relief model in the municipal museum. But once we recover our breath it is clear that we have *already* gone wrong. That is impressive. We must have missed, while gasping for air, the familiar acorn sign that would have directed us around Prestatyn Hillside to the west. But we have got our official viewpoint (probably intended for motorists and coach parties) on the wrong side of the hill and there's a Celtic cross thrown in as well. And do we care?

After plunging along some minor footpaths and crossing some empty lanes we are soon back on track and the cool, clean spring air is delicious and vivifying. Later, the path comes very close to St Beuno's, a rather forbidding, cold grey place, the Jesuit training college where the poet Gerald Manley Hopkins came to study theology for four years in the 1870s. It is smothered in "Private" signs and surrounded by a moat of wild garlic just about to break out into its delicate, serrated white flower. Part of me is tempted to trespass, with a pre-prepared script of politely apologetic confusion if challenged by some stern Jesuit patrol, but another part of me taps into old ambivalences rooted in my Catholic childhood that make me want to steer away from this place (its architect was Hansom who invented the cab). That greying limestone, its hard dullness, speaks to me of institutions, religious buildings where I felt hemmed and constrained, gasping for spiritual breath. That shiny new garlic leaf, too, reminds me also of the reality that Hopkins, with his minute Ruskinian devotion to the face of nature that gave us those extraordinarily detailed verbal notations that fill the published journals and letters, felt that he had to murder his gift here, to suppress with typically scrupulous Victorian hyper-religiosity – what his biographer Norman White in his little book on Hopkins in Wales calls "puritanism" – his poetic temperament. Poetry is written by people in love with the sensuousness of things and of language and Hopkins felt that mortification of the flesh (there was only one bath at St Beuno's and a shaky central heating system) was a necessary part of his preparation to serve God, of the imperative to embrace the rigorous spiritual discipline of the Jesuit codes. Fortunately, another part of his spirit resisted and some of his best and most beautiful poetry that celebrates 'pied beauty', the glory of the earth's variousness and contrasts, was written here at St Beuno's. And the most famous poem of all, *The Wreck of the Deutschland*, had its difficult birth at the house.

Hopkins arrived at St Beuno's on 28th August 1874, having been met at St Asaph and taken by pony and trap to the house where a vase of scarlet geraniums had been put out to welcome him in his room. The blooms would lighten the gloom of the iron bedstead over which a crucifix was nailed, the chamber-pot, and dark brown chest of drawers. It was still the summer holidays until 2nd October and the first weeks were relatively undemanding, with fewer people than usual about. He immediately wrote to his family in Hampstead, who had been far from happy at his conversion to Catholicism, to describe his arrival and to explain that his ordination was going to be sooner than he had previously expected. His family and friends like the poet Robert Bridges persistently failed to spell either "St Beuno's" or "St Asaph" correctly. It was, after all, in Wales. "The house stands on a steep hillside," he told his father the next day, "it commands the long-drawn valley of the Clwyd to the sea, a vast prospect, and opposite is Snowdon and its range, just now it being bright visible but coming and going with the weather. The air seems to me very fresh and wholesome." Hopkins was bracing himself for some "very close" hours of study, "lectures in dogmatic theology, moral ditto, canon law, church history, scripture, Hebrew and what not". He was also trying to come to terms with Hansom's architecture: "It is built of limestone, decent outside, skimpin within, Gothic, like Lancing College done worse. The staircases, galleries, and bopeeps are inexpressible: it takes a fortnight to learn them. Pipes of affliction convey lukewarm water of affliction to some of the rooms, others more fortunate have fires." Hopkins assumed he would be at St Beuno's for four years but in fact stayed until 19 October 1877, just over three years.

The surrounding countryside and the natural prospect of St Beuno's was more to Hopkins's taste: "The garden is all heights, terraces, Excelsiors, misty mountain tops, seats up trees called Crows' Nests, flights of steps seemingly up to heaven lined with burning aspiration upon aspiration of scarlet geraniums: it is very pretty and airy but it gives you the impression that if you took a step farther you would find yourself somewhere on Plenlimmon, Conway Castle, or Salisbury Craig."

Hopkins had barely arrived when he realised another very

important thing about the position of St Beuno's: it was in Wales. "I have half a mind to get up a little Welsh," he wrote on his first day, "all the neighbours speak it." He would indeed devote himself to learning Welsh without ever achieving the fluency that George Borrow, whom we will meet shortly, claimed for himself. His lack of ease with ordinary people, no doubt exacerbated by the position and general air of Englishness of this contained Jesuit community, wouldn't have helped his conversational Welsh. Tavern-chatter of the kind Borrow relished would be equally out of the question.

His first days in Wales were spent, in spite of his general weakness and ill-health, in walks and exploration of the immediate countryside that for him evoked his difficult concept of 'instress', a kind of inner signature that landscapes write and which expresses their essence: "Looking all around but most in looking far up the valley I felt an instress and charm of Wales" he wrote in his journal little over a week after arriving. "Indeed in coming here I began to feel a desire to do something for the conversion of Wales. I began to learn Welsh too but not with very pure intentions perhaps. However on consulting the Rector on this, the first day of the retreat, that figure discouraged it unless it were purely for the sake of labouring among the Welsh. Now it was not and so I saw I must give it up." He also seems to have sacrificed his interest in music at the same time (helped to make the decision by the "grunting harmonium" in the sacristy which was the only instrument available to him). There may have been practical reasons for this as he was just about to embark on the ardours of intense theological study (and was due to start his first religious retreat in a day or two's time) so the Rector would have wanted him to concentrate on priorities. But the idea that philological study was not "pure" seems to suggest an excessively scrupulous temperament not unknown in that fervid atmosphere of High Victorian religion in which Hopkins had been immersed during his time at Oxford – he had actually been received personally into the Catholic church by John Henry Newman, the central figure in the Oxford Movement. Poetry too, the sensuous delight in nature and in rendering it, seems also to have been represented as a temptation for the pure soul to resist. Hopkins candidly told his own journal that the loss of music and the prospect of learning Welsh "disappointed me and took an interest away". He recognised that he was doing violence to his natural sensibility and in consequence "I was very bitterly feeling the weariness of life and shed many tears, perhaps not wholly into the breast of God, but with some unmanliness in them too, and sighed and panted to Him". Oh dear!

Hopkins recorded in his diary, however, that no sooner had he given up the idea of learning Welsh "than my desire seemed to be for the conversion of Wales and I had it in mind to give up everything else for that". But a moment's reflection on the rules of the Jesuit order as laid out by St Ignatius Loyola, especially in the area of what one was permitted to choose, told him that this was a bad idea. There is something very interesting in the notion of a middle-class Englishman from Hampstead, freshly converted to Catholicism, parachuting into the Vale of Clwyd where the dominant religion was very far from Catholicism, and resolving on a crusade to convert the Welsh to his new faith. He claimed, however, to possess a "yearning for the Welsh people" that compelled him to want to "work for their conversion". More than this, he told his mother around this time: "I have always looked on myself as half Welsh and so I warm to them. The Welsh landscape has great charm and when I see Snowdon and the mountains in its neighbourhood, as I can now, with the clouds lifting, it gives me a rise of the heart." Brushing aside the view that the Welsh "have the reputation also of being covetous and immoral" (he doesn't say amongst whom) he insists that he warms to the Welsh people "and in different degrees to all Celts"

When Hopkins calls himself "half-Welsh" – a claim, incidentally, that his biographers doubt, in spite of Hopkins being a reasonably common Welsh surname – he points to a very common phenomenon, what we might call "elective ethnicity". Just as some wish to dampen down any suggestion that they come from a particular race or nationality so others are keen, sometimes with scant justification, to claim that they are 'really' Irish, Welsh, or Scottish. Race prejudice runs in many circuitous courses and one person's desire to be thought a fiery or poetic Celt may be contrasted with another's anxiety not to be exposed to any disparagement of their

Celtic provenance. Something similar happens with class where the announcement that "I am working class" is often heard in surprising (surprisingly affluent) quarters. Equally, many are anxious to disguise what others brandish as a proud (if in their particular case historic) allegiance. We want to belong, in short, provided the membership has no disadvantages for us. Race, as I have already said above, is one of those liminal spaces where we struggle to define ourselves, to write the ethnic script that suits us, to indicate which side of the border we are on. In many parts of the world, of course, the distinction between one group and another is not a dinner-party affectation but a matter, plainly, of life and death. The desire of Hopkins to be seen as Welsh had very complex origins and may have been as much to do with his search for a settled personal identity as priest and artist and human being – with the attainment of a sense of belonging in the world – as with a specific claim on Welsh identity.

In the specific case of the Welsh community living around St Beuno's, Hopkins was probably right to reflect that: "The Welsh round [here] are very civil and respectful but do not much come to us and those who are converted are for the most part not very stanch. They are much swayed by ridicule. Wesleyanism is the popular religion." In some cooler comments on the Welsh he observed: "They are said to have a turn for religion, especially what excites outward fervour, and more refinement and pious feeling than the English peasantry but less steadfastness and sincerity."

Much more spontaneous and 'warm' was his response to the Welsh landscape: "All the landscape had a beautiful liquid cast of blue. Many-coloured smokes in the valley, grey from the Denbigh lime-kiln, yellow and lurid from two kilns perhaps on the shoulders of a hill, blue from a bonfire, and so on" is a typical journal entry for late September 1874. An Indian summer allowed Hopkins and a companion to bathe on 8th October, a week after term began, in the Holywell, or St Winefride's Well, whose healing powers he believed in implicitly and whose site was of great significance to English Catholicism and its history of persecutions: "The sight of the water in the well as clear as glass greenish like beryl or aquamarine, trembling at the surface with the force of the springs, and shaping out the five foils of the well quite drew and held my eyes to it." And it is clear that he did after all take lessons in Welsh, from a Miss Jones, who is referred to in his journal from February 1875, where they were translating the story of Cinderella – presumably not in order to arm him with the means of conducting a mission outside the Nonconformist chapels of Clwyd. He asked Miss Jones to tell him the Welsh word for fairy and she gave him cipenaper, related etymologically to the English word kidnapper, from the Welsh cipio, to snatch or whisk away. She added that she had seen fairies herself on the Holywell road.

On Christmas Eve 1875 Hopkins wrote to his mother, who had sent him a newspaper cutting of a shipwreck, that he was "writing something on this wreck", a reference to the genesis of his most famous poem, *The Wreck of the Deutschland*. "It made a deep impression on me, more than any other wreck or accident I ever read of," he told her. The poem also bore significant traces of Hopkins's exploration of Welsh poetry and metre (he had even tried his hand at composing a couple of short devotional poems in Welsh) and was justified in the poet's eyes by the fact that the Rector, when the newspaper reports came in, had said that someone should write a poem about the tragedy. Hopkins took up the hint. Although the poem is religious in its subject matter, effectively a story of martyrdom, which would justify it in his eyes, it has endured as an extraordinary experiment in language and poetic form that was remarkably innovative in its time. His St Beuno's friend, Clement Barraud, was typical of its first hearers in admitting that he "could hardly understand one line of it" and while acknowledging its power, he found it "rough and often rudely grotesque". Hopkins invention of "sprung rhythm" which made him feel it was necessary to add stress marks to help the reader capture his prosodic innovation was the principal cause of difficulty. It was simply not what a late Victorian English poem was meant to sound like – and for Hopkins sound was vital. He wanted his poems to be read out loud. He persisted and tried to get it published in the Jesuit magazine *The Month*, whose editor Fr Henry Coleridge dragged his heels because he couldn't understand a word of it and felt that he shouldn't be publishing a poem that made no sense to him. It would not be published until 1918 when Bridges brought out the first, posthumous, collection of Hopkins's poetry. The rejection hurt the poet and contributed to his growing sense of alienation ("To seem the stranger seems my lot") but he did not stop writing and it was during the period in Wales that he wrote some of his best poems such as "The Starlight Night", "God's Grandeur", "As Kingfishers Catch Fire", "In the Valley of the Elwy", "The Windhover" [a Clwyd kestrel], "Pied Beauty", and "Hurrahing in Harvest". The last of these, the last poem written before he left Wales for ever was, he later told Bridges, "the outcome of half an hour of extreme enthusiasm as I walked home alone one day from fishing in the Elwy". Another poem, "The Sea and the Skylark", which he said was "written in my Welsh days, in my salad days", came out of a brief vacation in May 1877 at Rhyl ("this shallow and frail town"). Hopkins did not like Rhyl, a town that today has few charms and many social problems, but we have the poem.

Ordained priest on 23 September 1877, Hopkins left St Beuno's a few weeks later for Derbyshire. He would never see Wales again and died of typhoid in Ireland in June 1889.

Another writer who left us his picture of North Wales, a little earlier than Hopkins, in the 1850s is George Borrow. Like most British travel writers Borrow was a self-dramatiser and weaver of traveller's tales some of which are rather hard to believe, especially in the matter of his mastery of other languages. As with Sir Richard Burton, another great 19th century traveller, feats of linguistic competence are claimed which, in a nation generally so inept at speaking foreign languages, inevitably provoke a sceptical response. The travel writer is, of course, the most unreliable of narrators, largely because there is generally no one else on the journey with them and so we have to trust them. There is no one to challenge their account. And so we accept Borrow's claim that he had learned Welsh from a solicitor in East Anglia and his Welsh groom, an ex-soldier called Lloyd. The poor groom was taunted by the English legal clerks and called Taffy and the famous rhyming couplet about the stealing of a piece of beef was regularly sung out by them. Borrow refused to join them in taunting the Welshman and instead persuaded him to teach him Welsh.

"He gave me lessons on Sunday afternoons," Borrow writes in *Wild Wales*, "at my father's house, where he made his appearance very respectably dressed, in a beaver hat, blue surtout, whitish waistcoat, black trousers and Wellingtons, all with a somewhat ancient look – the Wellingtons I remember were slightly pieced at the sides – but all upon the whole very respectable." Borrow, as a Spanish speaker, claimed to have no difficulty with the "ll" issue in Welsh which "is by no means the terrible guttural which English people generally suppose it to be, being in reality a pretty liquid, exactly resembling the Spanish ll". Like most Welsh learners Borrow found the grammar, especially the mutation of consonants, more of a trial than the spoken language, but he read a great deal of Welsh, especially poetry, and was "well-versed in the compositions of various of the old Welsh bards, especially those of Dafydd ab [sic] Gwilym, whom, since the time when I first became acquainted with his works, I have always considered as the greatest poetical genius that has appeared in Europe since the revival of literature."

Thus formidably equipped, Borrow and his wife and daughter set off from East Anglia for Wales (the other two really rather hankered after the fashionable spa of Harrogate but Father was not to be moved) on the afternoon of the 27th July 1854. When they eventually reached Chester, Borrow sent his wife and daughter on by train to Llangollen, which was to be their initial base, but he himself determined to make the journey on foot. Unlike the walkers I met on Offa's Dyke, Borrow walked in normal gear and not wearing the official uniform of 'outdoor' or 'adventure' clothing:

> *I bought a small leather satchel with a lock and key, in which I placed a white linen shirt, a pair of worsted stockings, a razor and a prayer-book. Along with it I bought a leather strap with which to sling it over my shoulder; I got my boots new soled, my umbrella, which was rather dilapidated, mended; put twenty sovereigns into my purse, and then said I am all right for the Deheubarth.*

First, however, Borrow visited a bookstall at Chester, picking out a book by the poet and archdeacon of Merioneth, Edmund Price, which caused the sceptical bookseller to ask if he could translate it. When Borrow did so the latter demanded to know what part of Wales he came from "and when I told him I was an Englishman was evidently offended, either because he did not believe me, or, as I more incline to think, did not approve of an Englishman's understanding Welsh". This was to be a constant theme throughout Borrow's journey. Far from welcoming his keen desire to speak Welsh, a minority of those he encountered were wary and even hostile. What business had he speaking their language? This is *our* language. In spite of his vaunted fluency, however, most people in north Wales could tell that he was not one of them. They tended, in his accounts, to assume that he was from south Wales rather than that he was English. Towards the end of the book he describes an encounter in a tavern in Glamorgan which he had now reached where the "grimy" company ask him if he can speak Welsh and Borrow says he knows the words for bread and cheese ("bara y caws"). At this the grimy pipe-smoker turned to his neighbour and said in Welsh: "He knows nothing of Cumraeg, only two words; we may say anything we please; he can't understand us. What a long nose he has!" Borrow sat happily in the ingle-nook to listen to their conversation and, after being called away to supper, returned to that corner later. They were now ready to interrogate him. Something about Borrow had raised the suspicions of the tavern company and they now asked him directly if he could understand their Welsh. His honest admission produced the following: "I will tell you plainly that we don't like to have strangers among us who understand our discourse, more especially if they be gentlefolks." They were unimpressed when Borrow retorted that any Welshman or foreigner could step into an English public house and no one in the indigenous company would care if they were heard by them. In the face of their adamant refusal to share their conversation Borrow announced that he would offer them some talk of his own and he started to describe his visit to Russia, which enthralled them. They pressed him for more and he told them of his travels in North Africa and about the Muslims who were "a people who live on a savoury dish called couscousoo, and have the gloomiest faces and the most ferocious hearts under heaven". Then he rounded the evening off, to the tavern's complete satisfaction, with a ghost story from Lope de Vega acquired on his Spanish travels.

Apart from walking and talking, Borrow's other great passion was ale, a jug of which had fuelled his discourse out of the ingle-nook. Nothing pleased him more than to arrive after a day's walking at some tiny house in the village that brewed its own beer. Once, he crossed a little stone bridge in the valley of the Ystwyth and saw "a small house on the shutter of which was painted 'cwrw'". He went in and asked for a pint of ale from the woman who lived in the house and who had herself made the drink she sold. After a defensive "Dim Saesnaeg!' she agreed, after he reframed the request in Welsh, to serve him. He was a hard man to please and found it a little too bitter and told her so. "Oh, for an Act of Parliament to force people to brew good ale!" he once begged on a day in the Berwyns near Chirk when he had been given inferior ale to go with his bread and cheese. His travels in Wales are peppered with accounts of the qualities of the local ale and his repeated rhapsodies make one nostalgic for the lost country taverns of the pre-supermarket-takeaway era that has seen so many public houses in the Welsh and English countryside close their doors for good. If you or I were to arrive at a small inn in the Vale of Clywd today no doubt we would find a half-empty parlour, a JCB driver in muddy boots punching the fruit machine in the corner, the bored landlady doing *The Sun* crossword, and a scatter of desultory drinkers scattered about the tables with frosty pints of lager, but when Borrow rattled the latch of a Welsh inn and burst in he always encountered pipe smoke and rich talk and as often as not some local bard or ragged scholar with whom he could exchange poetic quotations or recitations. He was unimpressed by the abstainers, telling a temperance woman in Snowdonia who offered him only tea at the end of his day's tramping that "you ought to be ashamed of yourself to have nothing better to offer to a traveller than a cup of tea. I am faint; and I want good ale to give me heart, not wishy washy tea to take away the little strength I have". She listened patiently then led him into a little parlour where she left him. She came back moments later with a tray on which shook a bottle of spirit and a tumbler. "I tasted it; it was terribly strong. Those who wish for either whisky or brandy far above proof should always go to a temperance house." By dowsing this powerful poteen with a jug of fresh ice-cold spring water he thus got his drink and escaped the peril of tea-drinking.

At the end of that first day's walk along the Dyke I catch a bus back to Prestatyn and the next day set off by car to explore the Vale of Clwyd a little more extensively than I could have managed on foot. First stop is St Asaph which is the smallest cathedral city in Britain. Nearly burnt to the ground in the 13th Century by the troops of Edward 1st and ransacked by the troops of Owain Glyndŵr in the 15th Century, the Cathedral was used in the period of the Commonwealth in the 17th Century to house farm livestock. I seem to have arrived on the morning of the patronal feast and the red-cassocked choir of fidgety boys and girls and some older men (slyly checking their smartphones) are in their stalls preparing to rehearse a psalm. The vicar (though in a cathedral I am sure he goes by another name which I would know if I had paid more attention to my Trollope) spots me sitting in a pew at the back as I examine the fine wooden ceiling. I think I know what is coming and, sure enough, the honeyed breath of Christian good fellowship is soon all over me. Although the Church of Wales is very much a part of the Anglican communion and St Asaph Cathedral feels just like a Church of England establishment the clergyman is of course Welsh. I note that the women have broken the Barbara Pym mould and are kitted out in white woollen cassocks and dog collars, relishing their recognised role in a more modern church. It's all starting to get a bit much, however, and I slip out into the churchyard where I spot the relatively recent black marble gravestone of the leading Welsh composer, William Matthias, a local boy – as was Henry Morton Stanley the explorer who almost certainly didn't say: "Dr Livingstone, I presume?"

As I wind through the Vale of Clwyd towards Llangollen I reflect that I am not really in border country, if that means being within a breath of England as I am at home in Radnorshire. But the local tourist authorities don't agree with me. In Ruthin I pick up a slick brochure called *North Wales Borderlands: close enough to touch* which points out that Liverpool and Manchester are only an hour's drive away: "So we suit the original thinkers. The sort of people who like to make their own discoveries. Because although we're close, we're different. Different country, different atmosphere. Think of it as life on the edge. Because interesting things happen where two cultures meet." There's a lot more in this vein and they are right that this is tourist country, with so many visitors from north-West England, as the Scouse and Mancunian accents everywhere confirm. This does indeed force one to think once more about Welshness and Englishness. Offa built his dyke to keep out the Welsh from his kingdom (if he did not build it simply as a piece of self-aggrandisement, to say *I can do this*) and the ongoing failure of the English to appreciate what is different and distinct about the Welsh, while seldom expressing itself in evident hostility, is still palpable. It is often a matter of language and my own moment of revelation came nearly thirty years ago, not long after I had moved to Wales, in the main street of Machynlleth when I approached a lorry from which vegetables were being unloaded. Two young lads had finished the job and were amusing themselves by throwing some residual bits of turnip and carrot at each other and generally skylarking about. As I drew nearer I could hear that the language they were using was Welsh. The penny dropped. Welsh was the natural and instinctive first language of these young Welshmen. It was not an affectation or a "survival". It was the living medium that they dwelt in. And this language, one of the oldest in Europe, is more incomprehensible to the average Englishman than French or Italian or Spanish, yet it is spoken everywhere on his or her own doorstep.

There are other reasons, of course, for the Welsh difference. Politically, there is more of a communal approach to civic life in Wales, something that the relatively minor devolutionary concessions embodied in the National Assembly of Wales since 1999 have continued to develop. It is a question of a culture determining its own priorities, making its own way, being allowed to act on its own choices.

Later than Offa, the Lords of what was known as the Marches of Wales or simply The March, ruled a space that was not so much a border or dividing line as a strip of autonomous country where no outside writ seemed to run. Reading about the mediaeval March provokes reflections on the idea of the border as a unique space in its own right rather than simply a fence to cross, a line of demarcation, a margin or limit. Instead of being either on this side or that side, one is, in border country, actually somewhere else that allows one to escape the idea of a totalizing allegiance. This makes it, for many a cultural outlaw, a liberating, stimulating, desirable space to inhabit.

As Robert Davies, historian of this time and space, describes the March in the 14th Century: "It had that exotic quality – once more compounded of inquisitiveness and fear – that all border areas possess. Here people of different languages, different cultures, different laws, different customs met." But for the vast majority of Englishmen, he goes on, "these differences bred suspicion and tension. Wales began in the March; and the Welsh were uncomfortably different, even strange. They were not to be trusted; they were, like acts of God, beyond even the guarantees of law...This fear of the unknown and the different contributed in good measure to the evil reputation of the March amongst Englishmen." This lawlessness was a matter of plain fact. The king's writ did not run in the March and so it was impossible either to pursue an offender from England into the March or to force an offender from the March to answer for an offence committed in England or against an Englishman. More than this, inside the March a series of lordships ruled each with its own system of justice run by the individual Marcher lord who had the power of life and death over his people. The March became a kind of launch pad for raids and kidnappings and merchants who were robbed while in this territory could expect no legal redress. Henry VIII's Act of Union of England and Wales in 1536 spoke of the general lawlessness of the lordships and the "dyvers detestable murders, brennying of houses, robberies, theftes, trespasses, rowtes, riotes" that were prevalent and "without punishment or correction".

It is difficult to connect this warlike territory, and its outlaw wildness, with the tranquil landscape of today.

The March was also difficult to define and many parts of it seem to have drifted in and out of England and Wales. Offa's Dyke or the River Severn may have been seen as the broad boundary markers but as Davies puts it: "They were figurative phrases for a boundary that did not in fact exist. Instead of a boundary there was a march." Contemporary records speak of, for example, Oswestry being in "the march between England and Wales". Radnor was included in the Domesday book as part of Herefordshire, but the powerful Marcher lord Roger Mortimer managed to challenge this and recover it in the 13th Century for the March, if not for Wales. These confusions persist to the present day, at the level of consciousness rather than geography, with many a visitor to the Hay Festival of Literature, for example, unaware that it is taking place in Wales. George Borrow famously asked a serving girl at the Radnorshire Arms in Presteigne whether she was English or Welsh and she is said to have replied firmly: "Radnorshire". I rather like that elective affiliation, that refusal.

Welsh was once widely spoken in Hereford but today the ubiquitous second language on its streets is Polish. Attracted by casual agricultural work on the fruit-farms the estimated 2,500 Polish migrants in Hereford and district are catered to by several city centre shops selling exclusively eastern European items – five of them remarkably in a short stretch of Eign Gate in the city centre – and although I have never witnessed any hostility myself there was an incident in the summer of 2012 when the "Welcome to Hereford" sign was defaced by racists to read "Welcome to Poland." This naturally attracted the interest of the *Daily Mail*, which found a local resident called, marvellously, John Bull, who said: "I think a lot of people are concerned that the town now feels more like Krakow than a traditional market town. There is a real frustration that the Poles are taking over the area."

As you drive out of the city of Hereford, past the SAS Credenhill Barracks where the guards at the entrance cradle automatic weapons, you are almost immediately at the church of St Mary, Credenhill, where the poet and mystic Thomas Traherne, whose acquaintance we have already made, was briefly rector in the 17th Century. This sweet-natured religious mystic would never have cradled a weapon of any sort. In his poem, "Wonder", about a world that is marred by its material obsession with "proprieties" (i.e. property) Traherne writes of how those proprieties are of no value or significance and how in his case they fled from what shone out "from the splendour of my eyes".

And so did hedges, ditches, limits, bounds.
I dream'd not aught of those,
But wander'd over all men's grounds,
And found repose.

Traherne, son of a Hereford shoe-maker, seemed to enjoy an ease of access to eternal truths and achieved great personal happiness in contemplation of worlds where "hedges, ditches, limits, bounds" had no point and where no borderlines boxed in his free spirit. In direct contradiction of Régis Debray's argument that borders and boundaries are useful notions, that distinctions work, Traherne here wants to dissolve all border lines and territorial limits. His metaphor deliberately confronts the reality of ownership and power which informs border-consciousness. His four examples ("hedges, ditches, limits, bounds") are specifically ways of parcelling out land to indicate where possession begins and ends and his spiritual aspiration also has a specific desire to "wander...over all men's grounds". It is a very rooted, concrete metaphor.

This quiet rural Anglican priest in fact begins to sound like his socialist contemporary, the Lancashire "True Leveller" or Digger, Gerrard Winstanley who in a more radical way advocated the pulling up of hedges and destroying bounds. In his 1649 pamphlet *The New Law of Righteousness*, Winstanley drew on the *Book of Acts* in which it is written: "All who believed were together and had all things in common; they would sell their possessions and goods and distribute the proceeds to all, as any had need." Winstanley contended that: "in the beginning of time God made the earth. Not one word was spoken at the beginning that one branch of mankind should rule over another, but selfish imaginations did set up one man to teach and rule over another." Using Biblical precedent, Winstanley argued that all men were descended from a common stock, and that there was no Christian justification for property and aristocracy. The recent Civil Wars which Traherne witnessed painfully at first hand as a child in his native city of Hereford, where the conflict was particularly bitter, were also very much present in Winstanley's thinking: "Seeing the common people of England by joynt consent of person and purse have caste out Charles our Norman oppressour, wee have by this victory recovered ourselves from under his Norman yoake," he concluded with satisfaction.

Winstanley's words are an echo of earlier radical English thought from the time of Wat Tyler's 1381 Peasants' Revolt when the famous couplet of the Lollard priest John Ball was written:

"When Adam delved and Eve span,/Who was then the gentleman."

Once again the spade, the instrument of manual toil, becomes an instrument of revolution, of communitarian claim to land and right. Winstanley and the Diggers in 1649 started a movement which involved seizing common or unused land in the home counties and in Northamptonshire, cultivating it, and sharing out the produce, to the horror of the landowners who hired thugs to beat them up. Their suppression was successful, since the government refused to side with the Diggers, but Winstanley continued to advocate land redistribution and a society of primitive communism without property or wage slavery. He remains an important figure in the history of English radicalism and his name is often invoked in socialist and green circles.

In his *A Declaration from the Poor Oppressed People of England*, he wrote: "The power of enclosing land and owning property was brought into the creation by your ancestors by the sword; which first did murder their fellow creatures, men, and after plunder or steal away their land, and left this land successively to you, their children. And therefore, though you did not kill or thieve, yet you hold that cursed thing in your hand by the power of the sword; and so you justify the wicked deeds of your fathers, and that sin of your fathers shall be visited upon the head of you and your children to the third and fourth generation, and longer too, till your bloody and thieving power be rooted out of the land."

This asserts an idea of land ownership as illegitimate acquisition, begun and sustained by violence, and thus not part of the natural order of things. And it is undeniable that fences are the first thing to go up when property ownership is being asserted.

But notwithstanding his very earthly metaphor the boundary that Traherne was concerned with as a Christian mystic was that between this world and the next, between the sensuous world which his poetry joyfully celebrates, and the world that lies beyond or behind it, or, more properly perhaps, *within it*.

In his great prose work, the *Centuries of Meditation*, Traherne begins by declaring that: "An empty book is like an infant's soul, in which anything may be written. It is capable of all things, but containeth nothing. I have a mind to fill this with profitable wonders." This wonderfully confident declaration of the possibilities of writing is followed by a promise that he will "utter things that have been kept secret from the foundations of the world" but once again this is not mere exalted woolliness. It is *this* world that is his starting point: "Things strange, yet common; incredible, yet known; most high, yet plain; infinitely profitable, but not esteemed. Is it not a great thing, that you should be heir of the world? Is it not an enriching verity?" The Hopkins of "Pied Beauty" could have said the same about that 'enriching verity' of the earth. Traherne wants to make his reader "possessor of the whole world", a kind of imaginative utopianism every bit as large-thinking as the social vision of the True Levellers.

What is peculiarly exciting about the poetry of Traherne is its eager embrace of the world and what he calls in one of his best poems "news". He writes in the Centuries: "When I heard of any new kingdom beyond the seas, the light and glory of it pleased me immediately, entered into me, it rose up within me and I was *enlarged wonderfully* [my italics]. I entered into it, I saw its commodities, rarities, springs, meadows, riches, inhabitants, and became possessor of that new room, as if it had been prepared for me, so much was I magnified and delighted in it." This is about as far from "joyless puritanism" (in a century that knew that commodity well) as it is possible to come. No thundering rebukes or prophecies of doom, instead an invitation to open oneself to the world in all its vivid beauty.

The poem "On News" is one of many "Poems of Felicity" which celebrate the child being presented with the knowledge of what the world has to offer: "But little did the infant dream/That all the treasures of the world were by." In Traherne's world we arrive ready to claim our entitlement of "felicity" and all we need to do is to open ourselves to it. In another poem, "The Salutation" the unborn child waits to be greeted or saluted by the news of what it is waking to:

> From dust I rise,
> And out of nothing now awake,
> These brighter regions which salute mine eyes.
> A gift from God I take.
> The earth, the seas, the light, the day, the skies,
> The sun and stars are mine; if those I prize.

To the rationalist mind, for which this is all mere words, such notions are no doubt vexing and a terrible betrayal of the scientific method of understanding the world. When Aldous Huxley, scion of a Victorian scientific dynasty, published just after the Second World War in 1945 his book on the mystical tradition, *The Perennial Philosophy*, that was precisely the reaction he provoked amongst progressive critics and reviewers who felt that the bold and challenging spirit that was Huxley in the 1920s had now succumbed to the temptations of the Higher Waffle. Huxley never minded his critics (who, had they read his previous work more carefully, would not have been so surprised by the new book) and in his anthology, touched as a result of the influence of his friends in California, by an Eastern bias, argued that the aim of life was to connect with the Brahman, 'the Absolute Principle of all existence''. The vagueness of such abstractions, the portentousness of those initial capitals, ring alarm bells for some, but the perennial philosophy has proved to be just that: perennial. Huxley was intrigued by writers like Blake who seemed to have some sort of short cut to other worlds, other realms of perception, and it was this that fuelled his famous drug experiments of the 1950s. A far cry from the "turn on and tune in" drug culture of the 1960s (which nonetheless recruited him as presiding guru, his image famously included by Peter Blake in his album cover for *Sergeant Pepper's Lonely Hearts Club Band*) this sober and tweedy scientific experiment in suburban Hollywood, described (rather disappointingly, I have always felt) in *The Doors of Perception*, was an attempt to cross the border between the world of daily reality and the world of the illuminated visionary. Huxley's essentially scientific and rational intellectual equipment tried its best but in the end he was not William Blake. But it was an important border for him to try and cross. He knew that there was something on the other side even if he could not possess it or adequately realise it.

Traherne's joyful intuitions seem to have come more easily and instinctively. He was a natural mystic, a dissolver of borders and boundaries.

4. The Village

After my walk along the border I am back home. For twenty five years I have lived in this small village in the Welsh Marches and I have still not worked out an answer to the question: where are you from? Where do you belong?

The Welsh flag in my neighbour's garden has been whipped ragged by the wind. It is flapping tightly against the pole and it needs replacing. I wonder if I should offer to chip in. In spite of flying from a private house it feels like public property, as if we are all responsible for it. I cannot quite account for the odd fillip it always gives to my spirits as I turn off the road by the village hall and start to climb the brief, steep stretch of lane that goes up to my cottage. There is invariably a strong and lively wind sweeping down the Radnor Valley and the vibrating red dragon on its green background seems to say something: this is Wales. It may be a handful of miles from the English border, and Welsh is not spoken here, but it is Wales.

Evan, in whose garden the flagpole stands, seems pleased when I tell him how fond I am of his flag. He tells me the story. Once upon a time they were all employed at the quarry that is slowly chewing its way through Old Radnor hill like a mouse gnawing at a piece of cheese. Then the quarry company told all the lorry drivers that they were no longer employed but had to buy their own lorries and sell themselves back to the firm as freelance contractors. Some, like my nearest neighbour, Dai, preferred to tell them to stuff this idea. He set up instead as a 'motor engineer', an old-fashioned term that you still see on the headed notepaper of garages round here, repairing and servicing all those freelance lorries. Evan still drives for the quarry and one day he noticed a flagpole in a yard somewhere on one of his trips. When the owner of the pole discovered Evan's interest he told him he could have it and it was tossed in the back of the empty lorry.

Evan erected it in the front garden of his bungalow at the bottom of my hill and I don't know how many flags he has been through to date, each whipped to shreds by the ceaseless wind.

You might assume that here in border country we are 'not really Welsh' in spite of the bilingual road signs. The true ethnic spirit is found – isn't it? – in the deep centre of a country, Wales *profonde*, not at these fugitive margins. Well, I think not, as I have argued above. It is at the sharp edge of things that the definition most effectively pronounces itself.

It's true that I have never heard Welsh spoken on the street in East Radnor (though the schoolchildren all learn it) but a few years ago when the Rhayader Male Voice Choir came to sing at Walton Village Hall (and a three-line-whip was imposed because it was a fund raiser for our own village hall) the evening ended with a singing of the two national anthems. Walton is even nearer than we are to that large ENGLAND sign on the A44 but the English anthem was despatched quickly and perfunctorily and then the Welsh national anthem was belted out in full. I looked around, embarrassed at my inability to mouth a single word of it, like a posh socialist at a Labour Party conference, moving his lips to pretend he knows the words of *The Red Flag*, and I noticed that everyone around me seemed word perfect and confident. Is this, I wondered, because it is the only bit of Welsh they remember from school? I ought to ask but I don't want to. I want to believe that it was a straightforward impulse of local attachment, that my neighbours feel themselves to be what they are: Welsh.

I have referred above to George Borrow's famous question to a chambermaid at the Radnorshire Arms in Presteigne in the middle of the nineteenth century as to whether she considered herself English or Welsh and her firm retort: "Radnorshire!" I have had identical conversations myself with my neighbours. You can walk out of Presteigne in a few minutes and over the humped backed bridge that spans the Lugg and find yourself in England but there is never any doubt that this is Radnorshire, though relatively few people in Britain have heard the county's name or could place it exactly on a map.

I used to be the Welsh Correspondent of *Local Government Chronicle*, a freelance job that took me all over Wales to municipal offices where I sat, taking notes, at the back of rooms full of local councillors where sometimes the only women one saw had come in to remove the tea trolley. This was the late 1980s and early 1990s when yet another local government re-organisation was being proposed. Briefly, it seemed as though a return to the old county map of Wales was on the cards, based on a small-is-beautiful philosophy, that would restore councils like Radnorshire and Flintshire as local unitary authorities in their own right. I recall standing in the small office of the Chief Executive of Radnor District Council and listening to a very convincing account from him of how this might work.

During my days as a roving Welsh correspondent the Council of Welsh Districts (CWD) meetings took place in the tiny council chamber of Radnor District Council in Llandrindod Wells (a town "equally hard for everyone to get to," one portly red-faced county councillor from the Rhondda once quipped to me as we stood stuffing ourselves at the free buffet in the shabbily grand Hotel Metropole that dominates the town centre). The district councils of course backed the idea of a network of small unitary authorities, though the Assembly of Welsh Counties, representing the bigger entities of post-1974 local government reform, and who met in the grander corniced surroundings of the Association of County Councils HQ in Eaton Square, Belgravia, disagreed. There is a tradition, particularly in rural Wales, of councillors running as independents. In England that designation probably means Conservative but not necessarily in Wales. I was in Eaton Square one afternoon when a Labour county councillor from South Wales made a sly dig at one of these "Independents" from a West Wales county. A railwayman, the latter turned to his taunter and said in a deep, mellifluous voice: "I was a member of the Labour Party when you were in short trousers." A ripple of laughter went through the room.

The CWD had done its homework, noting how small communities in the United States had run local services successfully, but the tide was running the other way and municipal *gigantisme* was considered the only viable option. Radnorshire, Montgomeryshire and Breconshire were thus dissolved into the vast Powys unitary authority which covered a quarter of the land mass of Wales (though certainly not its population unless you include the sheep). Radnorshire was allowed to keep its name as a "shire committee" of the larger unit but the idea of small, responsive localism died in the era of the founding of the devolved Welsh Assembly whose doors opened on 1 July 1999, the very day I handed in my cards as a Welsh Correspondent to try to earn my living full time as a Grub Street scribbler.

One morning in the village I become aware of furious activity at the bottom of the lane. "The Kinnerton Boys", a term which is used to denote the (far from boyish) male inhabitants of the village, have set up what amounts to a road block made out of bales of straw. It is the weekend of the Wales Stages car rally which will be passing through the Radnor Forest above the village in the early morning. Last time this went past we woke at four in the morning to discover a crowd of spectators, drinking from flasks of coffee and nattering under our bedroom window when normally the only sound we hear is the screech of an owl in one of the three towering trees (two sycamore and an ash) that loom over the cottage. Several smaller rallies have decided that the forestry roads are suitable for weekend rallying – and the privatised forestry industry is only too willing to profit from them – so on three or four weekends a year the peace of the village is disrupted. One is canny enough to keep silent because anything to do with cars is very popular and those who demur risk ostracism and disapproval. When he heard that a retired lecturer had moved in to the village Dai said to me in a confidential aside: "We don't like teachers." The explanation of this very unWelsh sentiment turned out to be that several years previously someone had tried hard to create a lobby to ban the rally. He was a retired teacher.

The hang-gliding centre in New Radnor also contributes its mite to the roar of internal combustion as the cars race up the hill on bright sunny Saturdays and Sundays to a launch pad up above on the Forest. Country pursuits, as I mentioned earlier, involve high levels of expenditure on kit – just look at the walkers and cyclists and estimate how much they must have spent on their machines and crinkly kagools and pricey footwear. They also leave a fancy carbon footprint as bikes and equipment are lashed to car roof-racks and driven here from London or the Midlands.

But I am puzzled by that road-block. Can they really get away with this? Do they have the authority to close a public road, which is what our lane is, even if it terminates eventually at a ford that can be crossed only by a four-wheel drive vehicle? It seems that they can and there is a great deal of bustle and animation and laughter at the checkpoint. Arriving spectators are stopped and turned off into a field where they can park after being relieved of a few pounds. There are no reports of any protest and at first light small platoons of unhorsed motorists start to toil up the hill from the improvised car park.

The last bit of the ascent, just before the lane executes a sharp right-angled turn at our cottage is the toughest. In winter, when it is covered in a skin of snow or ice, ambitious motorists who think they can make it to the top often fail just here, on that last steep twist. One can hear their wheels spinning on the road surface. Once I slid back and the car turned a complete 180 degree circle before coming to rest gently on a snow-covered verge. Bins of salt and grit are placed at points along the lane and we occasionally go out and scatter a skim over the road at the turn.

Where the lane straightens itself again after the dog-leg turn it is level like a shelf, facing south east and drinking up the glittering early sun which makes short work of the frost on winter mornings. In the glossary of Radnorshire dialect in William Howse's *Radnorshire* (1949) "rack" is defined as "a straight path or track through the forest" which is good enough for me in trying to solve the etymology of Rack Lane. Standing on this straight and level stretch of road in front of the house (our front garden, on the other side of the lane, runs in a narrow third of an acre strip to finish in a tiny copse of small oaks, offspring of a massive 300 year old tree that dominates what we rather grandly call "The Wood", though it is just a small cluster of trees) the view is superb. Delivery men, plumbers, builders, on arrival at the property get out of their white vans and stand for a moment, dazzled by the generous panoramic view of the Radnor Valley and

Old Radnor Church and, on the far side of the Valley, Hergest Ridge in Herefordshire, and, in the farther distance, when not obscured by mist, the sometimes surprisingly sharply etched contours, in sunlight, of the Black Mountains beyond Hay-on-Wye.

Standing there on an autumn morning in the cold, beautiful light one ought not to want to be anywhere else. One ought to be content, one's cup full. So why do I sometimes feel uneasy? It is easy enough to mock the smug triumphalism of the new ruralists who have 'found' their perfect house and location, leaving behind them the ugliness, the noise, the danger, the unpleasantness of the town and city, and who want to let everyone know about their good fortune. But they have a point. If you can manage it this has to be considered materially better than living in an overcrowded inner London street. I suppose I sometimes ask myself how it has come about. How did I get away with it? Or, more nervously at the beginning, like someone on a first date: is it going to work out? Can I do this? It is partly the sense of having crossed another frontier but it is not just the transition to another place. The boundary between the country and the town is perhaps stronger than that between two countries.

These are reflections that would not occur – of course – to the indigenous resident. I have been surprised, however, by their self-consciousness. They certainly don't take it for granted and can themselves be found drinking in the view, murmuring appreciatively about the beauty of the scene to anyone who passes.

The urban fear – or mild anxiety – about the countryside makes sense even if one doesn't actually share it oneself. The absence of noise, for example, is a delight to me but it may feel disquieting to others for whom noise is a comfort, a reassurance, a reminder that other people exist and are not far away. I know that there are those who find the total, drenching silence, and the absence of artificial light outside, unsettling. What is out there? The rustlings and animal cryings, the flittings in the dark, convey a sense of menace to them. But the worst that has happened to me was to be stung on the crown of my head in the night one September when a somnolent wasp that must have flown in through the open window during the day and established itself somewhere beneath the pillow exacted a penalty from me for having been disturbed. And it could have happened in Ball's Pond Road.

If I am occasionally restless here, not quite at ease, it is not the result of these unnamed fears or of feeling an intruder, a person 'from off' as the local idiom has it, an *illegale*, or a wetback, like the Moroccans who have shinned over the Melilla fence. Nor is it the result of practical obstacles and inconveniences though these have to be admitted: the vestigial public transport, the fact that one must drive several miles to do something as simple as purchase a daily newspaper, the harshness of winter. Without mains sewerage one has even to remember to check that the septic tank does not need emptying. This is done by a large tanker that, every few years, comes to suck out the months of part-composted human waste. Living in a serviced mansion block in Central London – as I do for a part of my life – one is relieved of all this strenuous daily effort just to make things work, happy to listen contentedly to the smooth hum of an efficient machine for living. No, it is none of these things that passes through my mind as I crunch the autumn leaves and gaze out from my shelf of land. I grope to define it. Possibly it is a doubtful, hesitant sense that in the second decade of the 21st Century, in an epoch of global flight from the land to the city, when even traditional agriculture is here only because it is kept officiously alive, living in the country can sometimes feel like a wilful rejection of contemporary reality or a cop-out.

The most commonly used term to describe a move to the country is still 'escape'.

I try to understand the people I have come among, the border people whose territory I now share

I am constantly told by my neighbours that winters are not as harsh as they used to be. Whether this is a direct result of the warming of the planet or whether climate change is merely causing cyclical disruptions of the normal weather patterns, the undeniable fact is that, in the quarter of a century that I have lived in this valley, I have seen less and less snow. At the same time we have had some savage episodes of cold. In December 2010, the recorded official temperature at Builth Wells one night was minus 30 degrees. At the heart of my boiler something died and pipes fissured and that Christmas Day I washed in melted snow, having no running water. On the day after Boxing Day we made an excursion to the swimming pool at Ludlow in order to use its showers. Our reward, of course, was skies of perfect blue and the glittery sparkle of sunshine on the frozen drifts of snow.

Meanwhile my neighbours talk of a time when they regularly walked in deep drifts over the tops of hedgerows and when the snow lay on the fields for weeks on end.

Snow has its compensatory dramas; the grey, dark midwinter days are another matter. Sometimes, in the early weeks of February, on a day when the harsh cold is not even relieved by winter sunshine, there is a bitter, unrelenting, feel to the weather. In a corner of The Wood the snowdrops may be pushing their green spikes through the mat of frozen leaf and dead grass, and if one looks carefully there are buds prepared to break out on some of those bare branches, perhaps even the first hint of the daffodil tips that will erupt in an orchestra of yellow trumpets in a month's time, but there remains something implacable at the heart of these winter days.

Today I force myself to take a walk in the teeth of a biting wind and some stinging flakes of sleet. It is not yet four in the afternoon but it seems to be getting dark. Half way down the hill I see a tractor coming towards me, driven by the son of the farmer who owns most of the fields below and around us. He is crouched grimly over the wheel, a great green hooded oilskin draped over him so that I can barely see his face under its glistening monkish cowl. We exchange muted, shivering gestures of greeting and I turn to watch the tractor grind slowly up the hill behind me.

What kind of life is this for a young man, his contemporaries partying and clubbing and tapping away at Facebook pages which our internet connections at this stage (later, download speeds will catch up) would render problematic? He must get up early regardless of the weather, work seven days a week, set his face to the east wind, and often engage in hard back-breaking work after slipping from the sacking-lashed seat of that tractor to the ground. So much of this work, too, is solitary. It seems a tough, and unforgiving life for a young man (though no doubt he will inherit the considerable land and property that this father and mother own) and one that cannot allow him much of a social life with young people of his own age.

Two weeks later, I am sitting comfortably in front of the wood-burning stove, shaking out the latest issue of the *Brecon and Radnor Express* and my eye falls on a photograph of my tractor driver. In a sparkly waistcoat he is identified by the caption as Radnor Young Farmers' Disco Dancing Champion of the Year.

I have got it wrong again.

It is another morning of limpid beauty. Just before dawn, pools of white mist lay in the valley and above the ridge of Hergest the sky was garishly aflame. Then the sun's disc appeared, quickly establishing its authority and soaking into itself all of that colour in order to prepare the way for a sky of unflecked blue.

It has been a clear cold night of almost-frost and the grass is heavy with dew, glinting in the sun. Last night Derek, the faintly camp weather forecaster on BBC Wales, predicted thick fog but as the day emerges it is clear as a glittering stream. I stand in front of the cottage, breathing in that deliciously cold, fresh, pure air. The leaves on the late October trees are pale gold and the sun warm on my face.

I walk down the hill just after nine to catch the bus to London. A slight exaggeration: I must change buses twice and trains twice but I will be in London by 2.30 in the afternoon. Only one bus a day in the direction of Hereford passes through the village, all the others choosing a route which would entail a two mile walk to that main road where you flag the bus down or, if you are coming from the other direction, ask to be put off there.

As I wait at the bus stop I notice that it is steaming as if it were a smouldering log. I am too early (can't be too careful because the bus whizzes past and probably isn't expecting anyone to be standing at the stop) so I pull open the door of the phone box. It's one of those ancient red phone boxes that got overlooked when they were replacing them with new glass and steel versions, and I peer idly inside. There's a sign warning that in this "building" no one must smoke. But only spiders seem to use it now. You can no longer make a call using coins, only with a credit card, which will put off the older, poorer villagers who might be precisely the ones who would still make use of it. Another sign from British Telecom sternly announces that the box is to be disconnected because it is not being used with sufficient regularity. The local community may "adopt" it on payment of £1 and preserve it for "heritage" purposes. I don't know whether this has happened and I make a mental note to inquire.

It would be nice to keep it as a memorial to ancient days when people stepped inside a phone box (as I have done frequently when my line has stopped working and I have had to come down the hill to complain to the telephone company) and let their coins clatter through the box when the "pips" went. I remember as a child the box opposite our suburban house where we would play at pushing in pennies (yes, those big brown circular things that you see at car boot sales) and press Button B to retrieve them. The explanation for the decline of the phone box isn't hard to work out, especially as most of the mobile phone companies now provide at least a basic service in the Radnor Valley, but it is sad to see the red paint flaking off and the air of neglect and abandonment settling over this iconic feature of the man-made rural landscape.

The centre of the village is uncannily quiet most of the time. There is no pub or shop (though one of the cottages carries a painted sign memorialising "Ye Olde Shoppe") and even the church which dominates the centre from its mound is part of a group of parishes that desperately try to fill their pews in rotation each Sunday. The vicar of nearby New Radnor, an American, long gone, who used to drive a puttering Citroen 2CV, years ago explained to me that when the Church of Wales was disestablished in 1920 the border parishes were given a choice of which way to swing. It was a choice between the communitarian temper of Wales and the more conservative instincts of the English establishment. Those who chose to be with the Church of England had no taste for sharing the wealth of their endowments and our village was one of those. The church is now part of the Kington (Herefordshire) group of parishes. The vicar running the group will thus snake in and out of England and Wales several times on a Sunday. The most vigorous community facility in our hamlet is the Village Hall which is well-used and supported by a range of organisations including the Women's Institute. I once gave the latter a talk about my little book on Bruce Chatwin who wrote in *On the Black Hill* about the Marches – a little further towards Hay and the Black Mountains – and the speaker, by tradition, is invited to judge the weekly competition which was on this night for 'the most unusual object'. I cannot remember what it was but I suppose I must have made the right choice.

The village centre is a bit of a jumble. However much red tape the Powys County Council planners wrap around new building plans they never seem, in the end, to get it right. But perhaps it isn't possible to legislate for good taste and in the country the natural way of growing the built environment has always been the organic, bit-by-bit way. And we do have a village pond, restored and cleaned, on which ducks and moorhens glide. It is a quiet village where people mostly keep themselves to themselves and that is how they seem to like it.

While I stand in the sunshine waiting for the bus a small van appears at the crossroads, the driver pauses to scrutinise his Satnav, and then decides to turn left. The van bears the logo of Tesco, whose nearest stores are in Hereford and Ludlow and Llandrindod Wells, and it is bringing internet shopping orders to the Valley. I presume that this is why there is no longer a village shop and why the latest news is that the New Radnor shop has announced that it is to close for good. When I arrived in New Radnor in 1987 (living there for a couple of years before moving to my present cottage) there were two shops, two pubs, and a Post Office. In *The Shell Guide to Wales* (1973) by Wynford Vaughan-Thomas and Alun Llewellyn, published only fifteen years earlier, the authors write that New Radnor has: "a hotel and pleasant small inns". All that is left today is one pub, the Radnorshire Arms, whose future must be touch and go.

At last the bus arrives, swinging round the corner at speed. For a moment it seems that it is going to miss me and sweep on to the next crossroads, but it eventually comes to a halt by the phone box. I am amazed to find it so full. There is only one seat left in the 30 seater small bus that has come from Llandrindod Wells. It will continue through the twisting lanes until we get to Kington where we change to another for Hereford. This second bus turns out to be another small one, not really big enough, because by the time we get to the Herefordshire villages of Lyonshall and Weobley, it is standing room only, as if it were the London rush hour. Often on this route they run a double decker which is very popular with the schoolkids who go upstairs and make a racket as schoolkids must. The detractors of subsidised public transport – and none of these buses would run without subsidy – always like to claim that the buses are running around the countryside empty. It is true that in the past I have been the sole passenger on some stages of the journey but generally the services seem well-used. I then think of the billions of pounds of public money spent annually on motorway-building, on traffic police with their massive Range Rovers and whirring helicopters and state of the art control rooms, on costly emergency ambulances scraping drivers off the tarmac, and on constant maintenance of verges and surfaces and signs, and I conclude that the petty subsidies to rural transport are easily justified. Though most of my friends don't use the bus – there is a class issue here I suspect as well as their car-addiction – they are a vital part of the rural infrastructure for those who do. I only wish that those responsible for tourism would wake up and start advertising and promoting these services, letting walkers in the cities know that they don't need to bring their car with them. How often have I seen out of date bus timetables fixed to bus stops and even inside the public libraries. You need to know that you can walk from central London to the Radnor Forest without once jangling a set of car keys.

At Hereford I am dropped outside the station and, half an hour later, the train to Carmarthen pulls in and I catch it as far as Newport.

Waiting for the high speed train that will take me on the final stage of the journey to Paddington, I reflect that today's five hour journey from the Marches is slightly longer than the train from St Pancras to Avignon advertised on the London Underground.

I look along the platform at Newport and recall that it was here a decade or so ago that I spotted one afternoon an elderly man in a donkey jacket, with streaming white hair, apparently talking to himself and swirling his stick around in a rather alarming fashion. A woman with a small child got up from her bench and came over to him. She seemed to want the eccentric fellow to see the child – as if she were one of the devout seeking the blessing of a religious guru. Then I realised who it was and that she wanted the boy to grow up saying he had shaken hands with the much revered Member of Parliament for Ebbw Vale, Michael Foot.

Having come to live here directly from London, though not a native of that city, I am one of that group of incomers known as "people from off", a phrase that has no overtone of hostility or resentment. Radnorshire people are friendly and accommodating, perhaps because they sense that they are in no danger of being swamped by a tide of incomers. The demographic balance is in their favour. Our little village is typical in welcoming newcomers but the councillors and community councillors are entirely of indigenous stock. It is the first community I have lived in where one's arm has not been twisted to stand for this and that – though we do our bit to support village hall fund-raising events. I find this a very civilised way of proceeding. People respect one another, have no difficulty in sensing where minor and unimportant boundaries run, have the measure of one another, and are always polite and courteous and have the time of day to spare but are not prying or intrusive. No frontier rituals require to be observed.

We arrived first in New Radnor, a little over two miles away, in the autumn of 1987. I can hardly believe it is a quarter of a century ago. We had been slow driving down from London and the removal men were kicking their heels, waiting to be let in. We had hardly been there half an hour before Hilary from the little village shop and bakery opposite (all now vanished) came across with a tray of tea and biscuits and introduced herself. The house on the corner had been empty for a few years and had originally been the village post office and before that one of the village's many inns. A small room with a window seat that faced the High Street was referred to by my next door neighbour, Mrs Griffiths, who had once lived there, as The Cider Room.

I am calling New Radnor a village but it was once the county town of Radnorshire and a lively market centre. Old photographs show market day crowds, a bull being led down the High Street, and women in long gowns and bonnets standing in front of our house when it was the Post Office. It was a nice big, light, spacious house but we sensed that, having come all this way from Bermondsey, we ought to be out in the country proper and eventually we moved to our current village, sacrificing space but gaining that famous view and a sense of peaceful isolation. Small villages can be noisy, especially when they have a pub (also long gone) that hosts Friday night rock bands, and community halls with rollicking rugby club suppers on Saturday night.

New Radnor has a castle mound which used to look down on our house but, to the great amusement of some visiting French children, who fell about laughing when they discovered that there was no castle to be seen, there is not a scrap of masonry left on this grassy hump. It was laid waste by Owain Glyndŵr after his famous victory at the Battle of Pilleth. Down the side of it runs a lane, rather like the one that leads up from our village to the Rack, that is called Mutton Dingle. It climbs up, ever steeper, to the Radnor Forest and beside it a lovely clear stream gurgles all year round.

I suppose I shall never forget the exalted feeling of those first weeks in New Radnor in the autumn of 1987. The weather was cold but day after day of bright sunlight and melting frost seemed a delightful gift after the stress and strain of London. I was exhausted by a decade of political and community activism, and the hard work of being one of the launch staff of a brand new weekly trade magazine in the social services. I had my fill of reaching Sunday evening with my batteries still not yet restored. Twenty five years on, this is common enough in workplaces which have become even more relentless and demanding in their appetite for the nervous energy of workers. We had at that time no email or internet or smartphones or laptops, just the first clunking grey computers which were little more than word processors – I had actually started my journalistic career on a manual typewriter – but the pressure of working in a small, understaffed, magazine office (where everyone smoked like tractor pipes, another quaint historical detail) was taking its toll, in spite of the excitement of being involved in a new venture.

Now, I would get up each day with absolutely nothing compulsory to do though there was a daily list of small tasks on the house to complete. I imagine that taking one's pension feels like this but I knew well that, at the age of 35, this was not an option – though I did receive a witty postcard from a well-known journalist friend who had just made a similar move to an Oxfordshire village. He congratulated me on my retirement.

We walked the hills or we gathered great basketfuls of massive white field mushrooms, *agaricus campestris*, their fresh pink undersides wet with dew and with wisps of grass adhering. Never again over the subsequent two decades would we see such a freak crop. One morning a farmer's wife appeared in the field, gesticulating grumpily, as if we were stealing her livelihood, but there were so many mushrooms that autumn that they were rotting and turning black and shrivelled, unpicked in the fields. What overwhelmed me in that enchanted time was the air: so clean, and sharp and pure. I had left a Georgian house in a scruffy Bermondsey street where bus passengers turned their heads and looked blandly through our windows, where the traffic groaned day and night, and where the paintwork of the front door was covered in a noxious, metallic dust, borne on stale air foul with carbon monoxide fumes. I hope no one saw me in the back garden in those first weeks in New Radnor, taking great gulps of air like a desert traveller who has finally reached the oasis and is quenching an intolerable thirst.

There was a sense of freedom, of newness, of release, of anticipatory excitement, that I know I will not feel again with a comparable intensity, whatever adventures are left in store for me.

Yes of course, I was 'from off'. I had no illusions about belonging, about becoming naturalised, and I didn't care a fig about being 'accepted'. I was content simply to be here. A quarter of a century on I am still here, however often work and the need to travel take me away. The world, too, is larger than any village and I want to see more of it, but this is (if anything can be) home, the centre to which one returns, the place that waits patiently for the restless spirit to settle itself and be still. I think this is a good enough reason to cross a frontier: to see if things are greener on the other side. It is too soon to say, but it looks as though they might be.

I began by saying that I wrote this book in order to explore a feeling I have always had that a border runs through my own self, that I was divided, not an easy belonger, preferring the fugitive margins of border country to the confident claim to a single, definite patch of turf in the centre of things.

That will always be the case so it's best to make a virtue of it, to relish the shiftings and shadings, the shy arrivals and disappearances, the liberating ambiguities and ambivalences, of the liminal.

Also by the author

Real Bloomsbury
by Nicholas Murray
Sereies editor: Peter Finch

Pb £9.99
Seren 2010
ISBN: 9781854115263

Birthplace of Christian Socialism. Site of the British Museum, University College, RADA, the Friends House, the BMA, Great Ormond Street Hospital. Bloomsbury is crammed with history and with contemporary decision-making. But there is also working class Bloomsbury and, now, Bengali Bloomsbury in the east.

Biographer and novelist Nicholas Murray walks this crowded square mile or so, among the locals, the students, the tourists, alone or in the company of local characters, to give Bloomsbury the 'Real' series treatment of history, memoir, 'psychogeography' and oblique approaches to the familiar. His entertaining and informative text is accompanied by equally oblique images, the sort you won't find in either tourist guides or regular history books. All of which present Bloomsbury as it's never been portrayed before: intimate, contemporary, exploratory and occasionally downright strange.

Remembering Carmen

by Nicholas Murray

Pb £6.95
Seren 2003
ISBN: 1854113372

Nicholas Murray's second novel is an elegant dissection of modern romantic mores. Christopher, a successful shopfitter specialising in transforming dilapidated London buildings into swanky bistros, is romantically involved with Carmen, a one-time academic now unhappily employed as a magazine-columnist. Jimmy, millionaire and virtuoso pianist with a laissez-faire attitude to life, seems to offer the fullfillment she seeks.

Remembering Carmen takes the form of Christopher's 'memorial' to his former love. Set in London, Nice, the Greek Isles and Tuscany, it is a beautifully-crafted and utterly convincing portrait of adultery and its repercussions. Murray tracks his characters through the worlds of classical music, journalism, fashion-modelling and architecture, and asks where contentment might be found in an increasingly complex yet superficial world. His is a humane, concise voice, informed by European culture yet soberly grounded in modern Britain; *Remembering Carmen* consolidates Nicholas Murray's position as one of our most insightful and original new novelists.

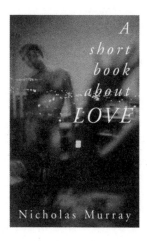

A short book about Love

by Nicholas Murray

Pb £6.95
Seren 2001
ISBN: 1854113038

Love in all its guises is the subject of Nick Murray's wise and witty *A Short Book About Love*. Woven into a comic re-telling of the classic legend of Tristan and Iseult - one of the world's greatest love stories - is the story of Felix, growing up in post-war Liverpool and, in the wake of a father's death, trying to come to terms with the meaning of what Philip Larkin, called 'that much-mentioned brilliance, love'.

In between are narratives, playful and serious, on the irresistible topic. This sparkling pocket-epic spans the globe, from Greece to Italy, from China to Russia, offering walk-on parts to Nelson Mandela, Clinton and Lewinsky, Oscar Wilde, Lewis Carroll and countless other poets, philosophers, and legendary lovers, who have learned that 'a world without love is no world at all'.